CLEAR AND
SIMPLE
GARDENING
GUIDE

CLEAR AND SIMPLE GARDENING GUIDE

BY D X FENTEN

Illustrated with Photographs by the Author and Drawings by Mildred Waltrip

Originally published under the title
Greenhorn's Guide to Gardening

GROSSET & DUNLAP
A NATIONAL GENERAL COMPANY
PUBLISHERS/NEW YORK

To *Barbara*
Donna
Jeff

For their love of life . . .
and me.

A 1971 GROSSET SPECIAL EDITION
Originally published under the title *Greenhorn's Guide to Gardening*

TEXT AND PHOTOGRAPHS COPYRIGHT © 1969 BY D X FENTEN
DRAWINGS COPYRIGHT © 1969 BY GROSSET & DUNLAP, INC.
PUBLISHED SIMULTANEOUSLY IN CANADA
LIBRARY OF CONGRESS CARD CATALOG CARD NUMBER: 68-15286

ISBN: 0-448-02445-4 (PAPERBACK EDITION)

ISBN: 0-448-01527-7 (HARDBOUND EDITION)

PRINTED IN THE UNITED STATES OF AMERICA

Contents

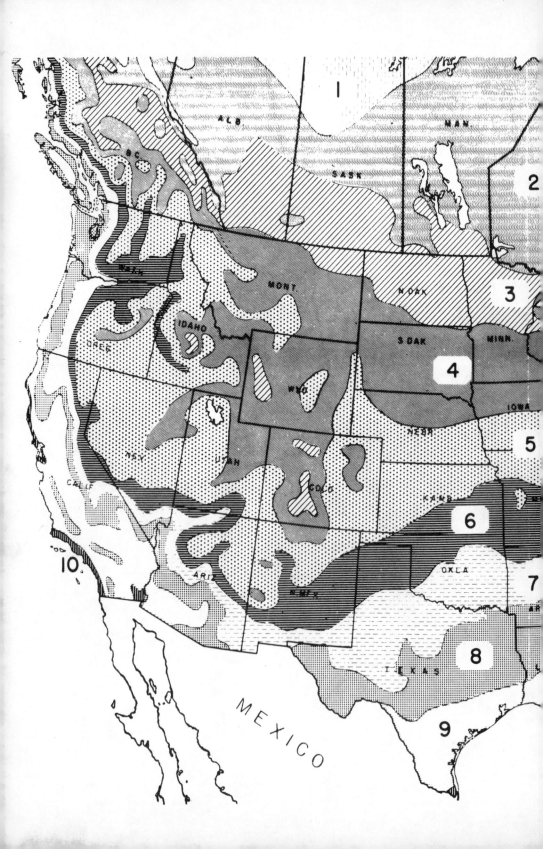

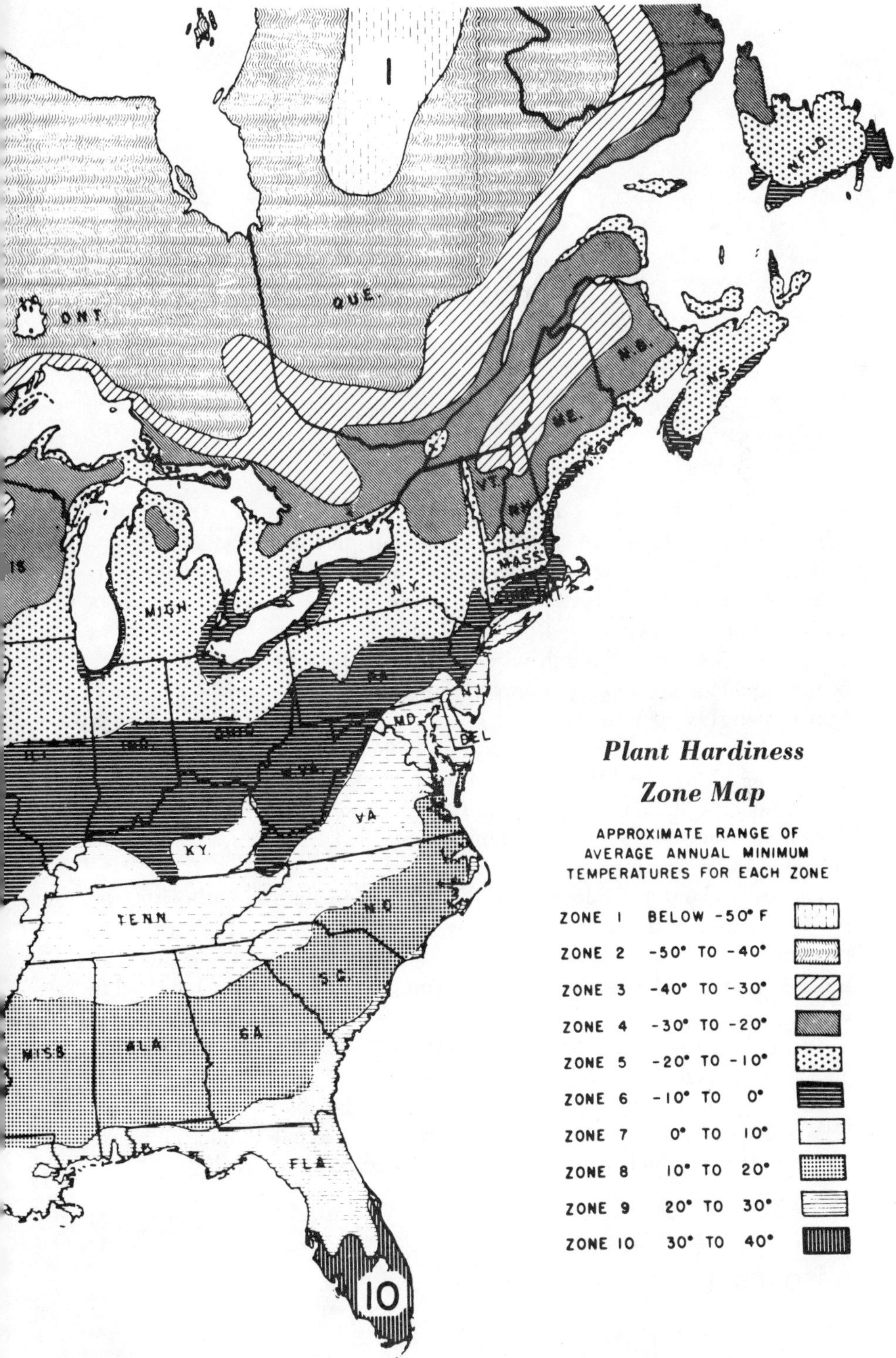

1
QUE.
ONT.
N.F.L.D.
N.B.
N.S.
ME.
VT.
N.H.
MASS.
N.Y.
MICH.
PA.
N.J.
MD.
DEL.
OHIO
IND.
W.VA.
VA.
KY.
TENN.
N.C.
S.C.
GA.
ALA.
MISS.
FLA.
10
Plant Hardiness
Zone Map
APPROXIMATE RANGE OF
AVERAGE ANNUAL MINIMUM
TEMPERATURES FOR EACH ZONE
ZONE 1 BELOW -50° F
ZONE 2 -50° TO -40°
ZONE 3 -40° TO -30°
ZONE 4 -30° TO -20°
ZONE 5 -20° TO -10°
ZONE 6 -10° TO 0°
ZONE 7 0° TO 10°
ZONE 8 10° TO 20°
ZONE 9 20° TO 30°
ZONE 10 30° TO 40°

Preface

Fall is the time to sit back and reflect on what has gone before and plan what we hope will be. Reflecting is pleasant, planning is vital.

It is now fall on Long Island and the sluggish pace of late summer is being replaced by the brisk step of people on the move. Homeowners and gardeners are rapidly getting everything ready for winter. Fall is not a season to be raced through without a good, long savoring of nature's beauty and, along with the appreciation of colors, textures and aromas comes thoughts of next year.

Completing a book is, to the author, like losing the last golden days of summer. There is little more for him to do but reflect on what he has done and start to plan the next one. Books, like most other endeavors are not one man jobs. Many people lent their time, talents and encouragement to this book.

The author gratefully acknowledges the help of the horticulturists, the growers, manufacturers and suppliers who gave their expert advice every time it was requested. To my family, friends and associates I can only say what I've said before—thanks for understanding when I say, "I'm writing another book."

To my mother, thanks again for everything which now includes faith and a professional job of typing.

To my wife, Barbara, who in fairness should be coauthor of this book, little can be added to what I've said before—eternal thanks and love for everything, which once again includes editing and typing.

D X FENTEN

GREENLAWN, NEW YORK
OCTOBER, 1968

Introduction

"He who knows what sweets and virtues are in the ground, the waters, the plants, the heavens, and how to come at these enchantments, is the rich and royal man," wrote Emerson. The phrase is apt, for very often we know "what sweets and virtues are in the ground," but even more often we do not know "how to come at these enchantments."

The frustration is great for most people, but it is especially great for a new homeowner and greenhorn gardner. Fresh from a city apartment, he realizes he is truly a greenhorn when he looks around the property he has bought and wonders "what happens now?" Where does he get the trees, grass, flowers and shrubs required to turn his house on a lot into a home with a view? And once he has all these green components, what does he do with them? How does he plant them? Feed them? Care for them? The scene becomes bleaker still the first time he walks into a garden shop or nursery and realizes how much there is that he knows nothing about.

Fortunately, no gardener, greenhorn or expert, is alone in his battles with and enjoyment of gardening. A recent survey by a leading tool company reveals that no matter how green you are at gardening, no matter how new at the game, there is always someone newer, someone greener. More than one million single family homes are built each year, all with at least a little land for gardening. Better than 205,000 retirees each year, or about 62 per cent of all retirees, turn to gardening as a hobby because it affords mild exercise, is constructive and offers an outlet for esthetic achievement.

Another survey, this one by a bank, gives an idea of how much money is spent each year on gardening. Would you believe that over four and a half billion dollars came out of the pockets of homeowners and gardeners for gardening needs last year? Or that the five million acres of home lawn swallowed up sixty-five million dollars worth of seeds and over two hundred twenty-five million dollars worth of fertilizers? How about the fact that four and a half million power mowers and 175,000 garden tractors were sold at a total cost of some four hundred fifty million dollars?

It is not difficult to see then how these surveys conclude that with eighty-one million gardeners in the United States "gardening ranks as one of the nation's main leisure time activities . . . with about one out of every two Americans engaging in gardening." Unfortunately, the surveys neither estimate nor put their computers to work to determine the portion of these expenditures wasted each year. They do not even try to guess how much grass seed fails to "come up," how many trees and shrubs are planted and then wither and die, or the percentage of flowers, fruit and vegetables that reach maturity only to be consumed by insects or diseases. They don't dare to estimate the losses in time, money and labor, but if they asked individual gardeners, especially new gardeners, they would find the results, or lack of results, staggering.

An almost uncountable number of books have been published throughout the years on each and every phase of gardening. This one, we hope, is different. It is written by a greenhorn gardner for greenhorn gardeners. The definition (according to Mr. Webster) should indicate the aim of the book and what we have tried to achieve: *greenhorn* ("a raw, inexperienced person—one easily imposed upon"); *guide* ("a handbook of information to direct the course or show the way to those following"); *gardening* ("the laying out or cultivating of gardens of herbs, fruits, flowers and vegetables; commonly such a piece adjoining a dwelling and enclosed").

Few preconceived notions remained intact after this greenhorn tried them out and watched the results. Without an inborn "green thumb" most new homeowners will find, as we did, that experience, rule of thumb and good old fashioned common sense can be considerably more valuable than all the theories propounded on the subject to date. Lest the reader be skeptical at some of the instructions or suggestions contained herein, let him be assured that they were learned the hard way, by trial and error—many trials and many errors.

So, if the surveys are correct and new homeowners "put gardens in the number two spot on the list of things to be done initially," there is little time to waste. Get out, get started, get gardening.

CHAPTER 1

Planning and Landscaping

"First plan, then plant" should be the motto of every new gardener and/or homeowner; unfortunately it is not. In an overwhelming desire to make his property "look nice" and add something green and growing to the barren wasteland on which he finds his new home, most new homeowners hurry about planting trees, shrubs, flowers and even vegetables in some of the most unlikely spots. Then, when reason starts to reappear he sees the error of his ways and realizes that less time should have been spent planting and more time planning. Then comes an awful moment of decision—does he dig everything up and start from scratch, breaking his heart and his pocketbook at about the same rate of speed or, does he attempt to salvage and rearrange?

PLANNING ON PAPER

Before doing anything definite, and to avoid wasting considerable amounts of time, money and effort, look at your property, at your home, at gardening and landscaping books and at other similar houses nearby where landscaping has been completed. A small amount of firsthand research will help you discover the requirements of your type of house, will indicate what is available locally and give you a good idea of what the landscape will look like when completed. Armed with this information, you are ready to consider the next steps.

Once again, enthusiasm must be bridled, for the next logical step is not to grab a shovel, but to grab a pencil and record accurately, on paper, all the dimensions and details of your house and property. Though it may seem simple enough to keep such details in your head, you will soon realize this is neither possible nor sensible. Using graph paper, ruler and pencil, carefully plot and sketch the outline of your property and then your house. Use a foot-to-inches scale suitable for your property and the size of the graph paper. For most simple drawings of this kind a scale of one-fourth inch equals one foot works out well, but for areas larger than one-quarter acre, a scale of one-fourth inch equals two feet is less cumbersome.

Orient your drawing so the house appears in the correct position on the paper in relation to the boundaries of your property. Use a large capacity tape measure or, better still, the builder's original plans or lot sketch and transfer all pertinent measurements and details to your own layout and plan. It is imperative that all measurements be accurate, for this is the plan on which most future work will be based, regardless of whether you do the work yourself or hire someone to do it for you.

With the outlines drawn in correctly and to scale, start adding as much detailed information as possible to your drawing—doors, windows, driveways and any trees or shrubs that may already be on your property. If there is anything else on the property, such as sheds, utility company poles or unattached garages, add them, in scale, to the overall plan.

Finally, check that you have everything on your property indicated on your plan. An oversight, sometimes even a small one, can cause considerable problems later. Even at this early stage, the new home-owner gardener should begin to understand the concept that the property, house, all improvements and landscaping are a complete entity—all the parts should, when you are finished, add up to a pleasant, harmonious and coordinated picture.

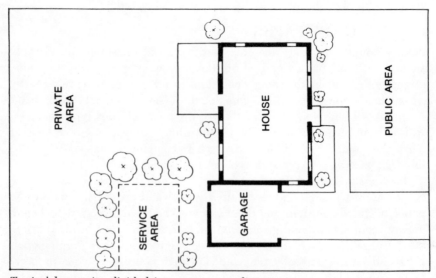

Typical home site divided into areas according to use.

Though few of us think of our property in terms of areas, the outdoor portions of our homes are divided into distinct sections, each having specific uses. The show areas are those first seen by your guests as they arrive (front lawn, entrance, driveway and foundation planting); the family areas are used by both family and guests but most often only by family (patio, children's play area, barbecue pit and flower garden); and the utility areas that are necessary but not necessarily pretty (wash lines, compost piles, vegetable gardens and tool sheds).

SHOW AREAS

Everyone is pleased when a guest drives up to his house and remarks how pretty it looks. Because first impressions are usually lasting, new homeowners are wise to spend much of their time, money and energy getting this part of their property to look just right. Also, it is the appearance of the part of the house and property you can see from the road that determines the tone of the entire neighborhood or development.

Lawns—Starting with a lawn that is green and well kept will go a long way toward setting off the house in the right light. If there must be a choice, for reasons of time or money, between a serviceable lawn throughout the property or a beautiful lush lawn in front and a lower grade lawn in other areas, strive for the best looking, most beautiful lawn in front. Use quality seed, and water, weed and feed as required.

Smooth, unbroken lawn gives fine first impression.

Care for your lawn just as you would the valuable possessions inside your house. Don't break up your lawn with a lot of small planted areas, but keep the lawn as smooth and as unbroken as possible. The impression of spaciousness makes most of the extra effort involved worthwhile.

When planning your front lawn, consider the problems of maintenance, especially mowing and trimming. Edging brick and other decorative elements add much to the looks of the approach area, but this decorative angle must be weighed against the amount of work required to keep it looking nice. Unless your mower can get very close to the brick, the time-consuming hand edging and trimming required more than offsets the decorative value gained.

Shrubs—Usually "type cast" as foundation plantings especially when they are used in front of a house, shrubs are quite valuable and contribute much toward making the front of a house look attractive and inviting. In this role, low growing shrubs blend the house and the lawn into a pleasant picture, hide the unattractive cement foundation, lead the eye to a focal point at the front door and add a distinctive beauty all their own to the overall landscape. However, this does not mean that a mass of shrubs placed along the foundation of your house will assure a nice looking entrance area. Shrubs must be selected on the basis of size, color and growth pattern, and then planted where they will do the most good.

Several simple suggestions will help you to get the most in good looks and serviceability from your shrub plantings:

1—Shrubs look best when single varieties are used alone or in clumps. Mixing shrub varieties detracts from all and leads to a messy or unkept appearance.

2—With the exception of particularly beautiful varieties used as specimen plants, use similar kinds of shrubs throughout your landscape plan. Specimen varieties can be set apart and "presented right" only when the eye is not confused by too many different kinds and groups.

3—Give the front of your house a natural look, at least natural to the eye. Plant tall trees at the corners and low growing shrubs toward the door so a graceful line is created, leading directly to your front door.

4—Though evergreen shrubs are most often used for foundation plantings, the addition of an occasional deciduous shrub, with pretty twigs and branches or fruit in the fall, can highlight specific points on your landscape plan.

5—The sides of houses can also benefit from the placement of foundation shrubs. If you have a long, blank side wall, use a clump of low

Without foundation plants this house looks naked.

growing shrubs to soften the effect. For tall houses, spreading shrubs, like certain junipers can break up the monotony and also provide a green background for other planting.

6—When planning, remember that shrubs need not be planted in single rows to be effective. For example, under the windows of your house put in shrubs that will grow to window height and no further or you will block out light and air and make the area look overgrown. In front of these shrubs put other, lower growing shrubs that flower or have interesting leaf color. The effect will be a smooth, pretty transition between the horizontal line of the lawn and the vertical line of the house.

Simple foundation planting ruined by clutter on left.

7—Don't limit the use of shrubs to foundation planting. Use them to provide a green background for a flower area, or for the flowers produced by some shrubs; use them as hedges or dividers between your property and a neighbors; use them to section off parts of your own property; use them as screens to hide unattractive views and areas used for wash lines, children's sand piles and other work or play areas.

Once you have learned about some of the many different kinds of shrubs that are available, you will be able to develop your own ideas for their use. Just keep it simple, don't crowd, and make it pleasing to your eye.

Trees—Planned and planted correctly, trees are invaluable to the homeowner who knows how to use them to his best advantage. Neither plan nor plant a tree according to the size they are when you buy them. Find out the mature size of each tree being considered, and the length of time it takes each tree to reach its maximum height, before penciling it in on your plan. A too-large tree, planted directly in front of the house, which may have looked charming when planted six-feet tall, may completely block the house in several years. Select trees that will give shade from the hot summer sun and plant them where they will do the most good.

Small tree off corner helps overall appearance.

Since trees are often used to frame a house, place them at the corners so the leaves, branches and trunks will have room to grow without interfering with other plantings and without overpowering the rest of the landscape. Check with local nurserymen on the availability and cost of the specimen trees or trees that are "different." Certain red-leaved trees such as Crimson King maple and purple plum can add just the right touch to your landscape plan and break the possible monotony of all green-leaved trees. Check into dwarf varieties and use them to accent areas where full-sized trees would be overpowering. Espaliered trees, in various shapes and sizes, are also worth investigating and will probably become the envy of the neighborhood.

Consider too, as you plan, that trees have a definite function as backgrounds. A few large trees, strategically placed at the back of the house, extending above the roof line will give the house a natural background, shade portions of the house from the blistering summer sun and also provide shade for a patio or other sitting area.

Like shrubs, trees can also be used as beautiful screens for unpleasant views. Check the views from your windows—if there is something that displeases you on either your property or your neighbors, correct placement of a tree or group of trees can often change a dim view to a bright spot.

Though a bit crowded, this planting is attractive when well kept.

Flowers—Flowers too have a place in the front of the house, but their use should be limited to highlighting shrub areas and adding spots of color to unbroken lines of greenery. The trick to correct use of flowers in the "show" portion of your landscape plan is to have them fit in so well with the complete plan they help form a unified and pleasant looking layout. For the most part, flowers, in foundation plantings, are best kept to areas between shrubs, in planters or in hanging baskets. Do not carve out a section of your lawn, plant some flowers and shrubs, call it a garden and stand back delighted with what you have done. An unbroken, or almost unbroken lawn line, leading from the street to the house is far more effective than small garden areas. Realize too, that most flowers, be they roses, bulbs, perennials or annuals only bloom for a short period of time and are not particularly attractive for the remainder of the year. It is far wiser to plan flower gardens for the side and back portions of your property than to break up the winning combination of lawn, shrubs and an occasional tree in the approach area of your house.

Though there seem to be many things to remember when planning the front or show area of your property, the key word in everything you do in this area is restraint. Keep the front of the house simple, well kept and uncluttered. Keep the lawn unbroken, the few trees strategically placed at the corners of the house and the shrubs low-growing, and the results will be pleasant to the eyes of all beholders.

FAMILY AREAS

If you start your planning for the family area thinking that your family will spend much of its outdoor time here, and consider it to be an outdoor play or family room, creating such an area will be quite easy. Probably the best way to start your planning is with a family conference. Sit down and discuss what each member of the family wants and needs in the way of an outdoor area. Consider each and every member, from the youngest who might want a sandbox or swing, to the oldest one who wants a shady spot in which to sit and read. List all the requests and when all are down on paper, start to place them in order of importance to the entire family, onto your overall landscaping plan. Some of the items for consideration within this family living area are a patio or terrace, barbecuing spot, swimming pool or wading pool for the children, sandbox, shuffleboard or other games areas, flower gardens, fruit trees, rock gardens, and if space permits, swings or monkeybars for children, vegetable garden, basketball rim for teenagers, reflecting pool and reading nook for adults.

Patios—The first item on the agenda for most new homeowners, when they start thinking about their outdoor living space, is the patio. This is the place for the family to cookout, to picnic, visit with guests and to ultimately enjoy the peace and quiet of suburban living.

When planning your patio, make it easily accessible to the house, preferably with a door from the kitchen or playroom (these are usually rooms built to take a heavy flow of traffic). If direct access is impossible, plan a short walk from the closest door leading to the outside. Be sure to put the patio where it can be enjoyed throughout the day. Placed on the north or northeast side of the house, it will get sun in the morning but will be shaded in the afternoon, the hottest part of the day. If the patio must be placed on the south or west side of the house, trees should be planted so portions of the patio will be shaded during the afternoon. Think big when planning your patio. Make it big enough to accommodate a picnic table and benches, lounge chairs and other outdoor furniture.

Consider the possibilities available for the floor of your patio—cement block, patio block (in a variety of sizes, shapes and colors), redwood, brick, or other paving materials. This is an expensive investment so investigate all the possibilities and then be sure when you finally choose.

A reasonably simple but good-looking patio can be made by placing patio block, bricks or other pre-cast materials on a bed of sand. Dig out the patio area to a depth of ten to twelve inches. Rough smooth and refill with six to eight inches of gravel. Smooth again and cover the gravel with two to three inches of builder's sand. Smooth and tamp the sand so it is as level as possible, with no bumps or low spots. Carefully lay the paving blocks into position, in the pattern of your choice, checking often to see that the blocks are aligned and flat throughout. When you are finished, use an outdoor bristle broom and brush sand into the crevasses between the blocks, and sweep the new patio clean.

Almost immediately after you have begun using this new patio, you will feel the importance of privacy, especially if you live in a new house where trees and large shrubs are nonexistent. If you use your patio for entertaining guests or just for quiet family reading or relaxing, privacy becomes essential. The proper screening material can give you the privacy you desire, provide a pretty backdrop for flowers, and shield you from strong winds and the curious glances of neighbors. Unless a swimming pool is included, it is usually not a good idea to use regular fencing materials around the patio. Vines hung on wire mesh or certain shrubs make excellent privacy screens. For the best results, when using a hedge or shrub screen, dig out an area all the way around the patio, about two and one-half to three feet wide. Plant the individual shrubs at the recommended distance apart, allowing for growth and spreading. After only a few growing seasons your privacy will be assured.

If your patio plan includes a sunken or above-ground swimming pool be sure to check the regulation in your township before proceeding. Many towns require special types of fencing around swimming pools and you might as well meet the requirements the first time without chancing having to remove and replace it.

Barbecues—It seems the dream of many people, when planning their family area, to include a brick barbecue. Here again, think before you build this large permanent piece of "furniture." With the variety of ready-made barbecues available, it seems almost pointless to go to the time, expense and trouble of building one. And, once it is built-in, it is a permanent fixture and cannot be removed or replaced despite changes in interests and activities. Many people barbecue madly their first several summers in a new home, but gradually, for many reasons, they taper off. Consider this possibility before building a barbecue.

Special gardens—Imagination, beauty and ease of maintenance should be the most important considerations when planning special gardens on your property. The gardens discussed in this section are those designed primarily for their color, variety and good looks. Any other gardens, e.g., cutting gardens and vegetable gardens, belong in a service or utility area.

As is true with all landscape planning, selectivity and restraint produce the most effective and beautiful results. When you first think about it, you may be convinced that flower beds completely surrounding your property or even encircling the living area would be a "thing of beauty and a joy forever." However, it may turn into a thing of beauty and no Saturdays or Sundays free forever. Unless you have unlimited time and patience for outdoor caretaking, flower beds are much more effective and easier to live with if they are limited to small pockets within a shrub border or in small independent curved sections. To look their best, flowers require almost continuous maintenance, trimming, weeding, and spraying. Roses, placed in a garden by themselves give a lovely effect, and allow ease of maintenance and spraying in a single compact area. To fill your small flower beds, to add sparks of color throughout your property and to give individuality to your landscape you can choose from a dazzling list of bulbs, annuals, biennials and perennials. Study the lists and catalogs carefully, choose slowly and effectively and, as you add to your landscape each year you will soon create just the right setting for your home.

Standing by themselves most flowers will look nice. However, if you plan to place them in your company area, you should give them company dress. By placing flowers before a special background: shrubs, a hedge, a fence or even a small wall, they will be outstanding in appearance. When planning flowers for display, consider when and how long each flower blooms. With careful selection you can have flowers in bloom throughout the major part of the growing year. Determine the growing habits and height of each type of flower and plant accordingly—low ones in front, tall ones in back. Position the garden so the flowers can be viewed and enjoyed from both the patio and house if possible, to afford you double pleasure.

Play areas—If your property is large enough, you may decide to plan the play areas so they become part of the utility area and are screened off from the other areas of the property. However, for those families with small children it is often better and safer to include the play area with the family area—close enough to the house to be watched from a kitchen or playroom window. If you plan to screen off this area with hedges or shrubs, either keep the screen low enough so you can see over it or leave the side closest to your viewing window open. Keep your children's play area simple and flexible, trying to think a bit ahead. All too suddenly children graduate from sandboxes, to swings, to monkey bars, to a basketball rim and then away from home.

UTILITY AREAS

These areas are best described as those you would like to do without, but can't. They are important and usually unattractive. They include: clothes lines or driers, garbage cans, compost piles, vegetable and cutting gardens, storage sheds, piled fire wood, and cold frames. Ideally, this area should be kept small, screened and neat.

Screening the area will eliminate much of the eyesore, but other little tips will help even more. Consider the new outdoor clothes driers, those with attractive canopies over them. When not being used for their primary function they look like and serve as outdoor umbrellas. Garbage cans too are necessary but ugly, so consider two possibilities. First, if you or a member of your family are creative with a paint brush, you can design and produce a colorful garbage can. One with large flowers, polka dots, or even a gay scene will add charm and interest to the area. The alternative is to enclose the cans in their own little shed (bought or made) which should be kept clean and freshly painted at all times.

Vegetable gardens and cutting gardens are not bad to look at if they are kept neat and weeded. Plant your rows straight and according to plan. Don't let weeds or rubbish accumulate. Mulch all around flowers and vegetables and do a little weeding each day. Maintaining these gardens on a regular basis will result in greater yield, nicer looking gardens and a considerably smaller work load. If you are planning a compost pile, sketch it in on your plan in some out of the way spot and screen it from view with a few well-placed shrubs. Don't plant the shrubs too close to the pile, but just far enough away so the pile can be easily reached and used, but not seen from the family area. A few shovelsful of soil on top of the pile after major additions of vegetable waste will eliminate most offensive odors.

Whatever you decide to include in your service area, keep it as small as possible, it will never be the showplace of your property.

PLANNING TIPS TO REMEMBER

1. Make your plan as complete as possible before actually doing any gardening. The location of such things as cesspools (don't plant trees, especially willows near them) and utility wires, are most important to the ultimate success of your plan.

2. Remember to plan for use and enjoyment as well as beauty. A too beautiful landscape that no one can use is virtually worthless. Combine beauty with utility and you have an unbeatable combination.

3. Keep lawn areas uncluttered, especially in front of the house where an unbroken lawn makes the most effective approach. Remember too that the lawn must be mowed so provide edging strips along which your mower can ride at the edge of each lawn area. Hand trimming is tedious and often unnecessary if you plan ahead.

4. Carefully research available trees and shrubs before you buy them. Color, shape, growth habit, maximum height and adaptability to local conditions are important to your selection and ultimate satisfaction.

5. Use restraint in everything you do. Treat each plant as an individual and do not crowd it out with what may soon become to much of a good thing.

6. Use as few drives or walks as possible throughout the property—they chop it up into segments and make the property look smaller. If you must have certain walk areas, pave them. Grass used in walk areas soon becomes worn out and run-down looking. Keep all walks straight and as short as possible.

7. Plan for adequate storage of gardening equipment, lawn mower, outdoor furniture, snow tires, etc. Many garages rapidly begin to

Low hedge of junipers sets off this house perfectly.

resemble Fibber McGee's closet. If possible plan to build or buy a storage shed and make some attempt, however feeble, to keep it neat and in order.

8. Check with your neighbors on their plans and work with them to develop a nicer neighborhood. If all can agree to keep fences off the front lawn, for example, the wide unbroken expanse of green lawn will be an added asset for the community.

9. Have your property surveyed before putting fences, shrubs or hedges near any boundary lines. Once surveyed, keep everything of yours within your own property—not on the line. (A friendly neighbor today can be replaced by one with different ideas which can include the removal of a fence on the property line, or shrubs or hedges which are encroaching on his property.)

10. Learn as many tricks and techniques as possible to assure minimum maintenance of your property, and plan all your gardening for the greatest amount of pleasure and the least amount of work.

11. Plan to enjoy outdoor living during the cool of a summer evening. Include weatherproof electrical outlets and garden lighting on your plan so you need not disturb lawns or plants to put in wiring at a later time.

12. Expect to use experts and professionals to do some of the work indicated on your plan. Know your limitations and call in professionals if the task is too exhausting or difficult for you. Doing it yourself

is fine for many jobs, but many others are not for amateurs. There is no saving in time, money or effort if the job must ultimately be redone by an expert.

13. Follow your plan and ad lib as little as possible. If the plan is flexible, it will allow for changes, additions and deletions with a minimum of effort. Disregard the plan you have carefully laid out on paper and you court disaster.

14. Don't try to do everything the first year. Follow a timetable (like the one offered here) and you will be able to enjoy your property even as you work on it.

15. Be patient. Nature will not be rushed. Realize that it will take several years before your newly-planted trees and shrubs "grow up."

16. Enjoy your new home and all your property—you've earned it!

FIVE-YEAR HOME LANDSCAPE TIMETABLE

First Year
1. Do all landscape planning
2. Take soil test
   a. Follow recommendations of soil test
   b. Add to soil so it has proper texture and chemical content
3. Put in lawn areas according to plan
   a. Level, grade and till as required
   b. Lime, fertilize, seed and water
   c. Maintain and fertilize lawn throughout growing season
4. Put in foundation planting
   a. Select permanent planting materials
   b. Plant shrubs and small trees in front of house
5. Plant trees
   a. Start planting trees according to plan
   b. Be sure shade trees are planted first
6. Put in patio or terrace
7. Put in sandbox, swings, etc.

Second Year
1. Maintain everything planted first year
   a. Fertilize, water and spray trees, shrubs and lawns as required
   b. Lightly prune trees and shrubs if required

2. Keep lawns weed, disease and insect free
3. Complete foundation plantings
4. Plant remainder of trees listed on plan
   a. Ornamentals and fruit trees
5. Complete and maintain patio
6. Enclose patio
   a. Plant shrubs, hedges or screen plants around patio for privacy
   b. Put planter or other decorative elements on patio
7. Start small vegetable and flower gardens
   a. Start compost pile

Third Year
1. Maintain everything planted
2. Plant any trees or shrubs on plan, not planted
3. Continue small vegetable and flower gardens
4. Start any new outdoor construction
   a. Swimming pool, patio awning, reflection pools
5. Start new special gardens or areas
6. Plant trees or shrubs to screen utility areas

Fourth Year
1. Maintain everything planted
2. Enlarge vegetable and flower garden to final size shown on plan
3. Complete and landscape all outdoor construction
4. Complete special gardens or areas
5. Train and prune shrubs and trees as required
6. Prune all hedges and screens

Fifth Year
1. Maintain according to regular work plan
   a. Water, spray, fertilize, cut, prune as required
   b. Add finishing touches and decorative elements where necessary
   c. Enjoy!

CHAPTER 2

Garden Tools and Equipment

In the hardware or garden supply store the new homeowner stands, bewildered, and rightly so. There are so many different tools available, and so many variations of each that the beginner just doesn't know which to select.

If he is like most of us, working on a limited budget, he'll want to buy those he needs, and only those. He needs tools and equipment to do the many gardening jobs around a house, especially a new house. He will want the tools he can use to do these jobs the best way—quickly and effectively. He will want tools that will last for many years and serve him well all through those years.

All tools, purchased by the new gardener, are investments, and should be considered as such. Buy quality! One of the best guidelines is brand name. One of the poorest is price. Never be guided by price alone when it comes to selecting a tool. Although there are exceptions, your best bet is to buy tools made by a company specializing in certain types of high-quality tools or those sold under well-known brand names. As a general rule, these "quality" tools are easier to use (better design), sturdier (better design and manufacturing process), easier to keep clean and maintain (better materials), and last longer.

BASIC GARDEN TOOLS

This list includes those tools which are used time and time again, practically every time you go outdoors to work. You can figure that you must buy: a shovel, spade, rake, hoe, trowel, pruning shears, wheelbarrow, hose, water sprinklers, sprayer and lawn mower. Not included are the tools and equipment for specialized jobs or those used infrequently and best rented.

Shovel—A shovel is a round-pointed, spoon-shaped tool. Because you will probably use a shovel almost more than any other tool, make sure you are comfortable handling it. Try before you buy. Lift it, and pretend to be using it so you can check the length, weight, and feel of it. Digging planting holes and transplanting flowers and small shrubs are but two of the many uses for this tool. The reason for its shape, and handle-blade angle, is to allow you to scoop up large amounts of soft earth and remove it, all without too much stooping and bending. So, unless you are very short, select a good quality, long-handled shovel for these jobs.

Spade—A spade is a flat-bladed tool, designed to slice into the earth and allow you to lift and turn over large clods of earth. With this tool, unless you are very tall, the almost straight angle of the blade and handle is best utilized with a D-handle. Better quality spades are made by attaching the blade to a metal shank (all one piece) which goes part way up the handle. Look for this when you buy digging tools, they last longer and allow you to apply more foot and shoulder pressure as well as leverage, when digging. These standard garden spades are fine for general use outdoors, but a nurseryman's spade has a smaller, slightly curved blade making it better for transplanting and other garden activities. Quality shovels and spades are made by such companies as Green Thumb, Stanley and True Temper.

Rakes—There are several different types of rakes, each one best suited to a different type of job. If you need a rake solely to collect leaves or grass clippings, a spring rake of steel or bamboo is what you should use. This rake is used somewhat like a broom, held lightly and "sidesaddle" and just swept forward with an easy motion.

Steel rakes are used to prepare the soil for grass seed, to level an area after the earth has been spaded, and to scratch-up hard packed dirt. Remember that both sides, the toothed as well as the flat side are used to level and smooth the soil.

Hoes—There are probably as many different kinds of hoes as there are gardening jobs and the difference is in the shape of the hoe blade. Select a hoe that is the right size for you. A hoe that is too big is unwieldly and hard to use. Garden hoes (flat-bladed) are fine for general weeding and for loosening soil.

Scuffle hoes are fine for weeding around plants and shrubs and also for many tasks in the flower and vegetable gardens. They are pushed back and forth just under the surface, as you back away from the area. The results are amazing—weeds are cut under the soil's surface and a smooth, even layer of dirt, without footprints, remains.

Warren hoes are heart-shaped and are especially designed for planting work in a garden, especially a flower or vegetable garden. The point of the heart is used to open up a furrow and, by turning the tool upside down, the "ears" are used to cover up the seed and refill the furrow.

There are other types of hoes available but they are so specialized they have little importance to the new homeowner.

Pick—This is one of those tools which should belong to the good-neighbor policy. Hope your neighbor is a good one, and has one. Its use is so limited, under normal conditions, that it seldom pays to buy one. Usually, if the ground is so hard and compressed that you need a pick to open it up, there is little sense in trying to plant anything there, it probably won't grow anyway.

However, there are times when the availability of a pick makes other jobs quicker and easier, such as digging out big rocks, small dead trees and large planting holes. A few well placed wallops with a pick make the job with the shovel a relative snap. A word of caution, if you have never used a pick before, don't haul off and let it fly like they do in the movies. You might be very surprised at the result. The one to go flying might be you.

Trowel—Probably the most used and abused tool in the gardener's kit, the trowel is used for almost any and all small garden jobs. When selecting your trowel, note the difference between the inexpensive and expensive ones. The difference in price is based almost entirely on mate-

Fine point trowel is excellent for transplanting seedlings.

rials and construction. Buy an expensive trowel, one made of a single piece of steel or stainless steel with a wooden handle driven into a socket and held by a pin. This type is the best because it is the strongest and longest lasting, making it worth the price.

Pruning Shears—Here too, there are no bargains. You get exactly what you pay for. Because you will continue to need and use your pruning shears for as long as you own a house and garden, buy a good one. To make those you buy last longer and serve you better, you would be wise to invest in several so you can match the tool to the job being done. The Wilkinson Sword Company make fine pruning shears, in sizes, shapes and designs for all pruning jobs.

For any pruning or cutting back of small-sized limbs (no thicker than a skinny pinky finger) regular pruning shears will do very well. For branches thicker than your pinky but less than one-inch thick, a long-handled lopping shear is the tool to use. For anything over one inch, steer clear of the shears, they will not be able to make a clean cut—so use a pruning saw instead. Among the finest pruning tools are those made by Disston and S. S. Smith.

All pruning tools should be kept clean, sharp and oiled, and should not be used to cut anything (string, wire, etc.) except branches and woody-flower stems.

Wheelbarrow or Cart—Useful for all the moving jobs around the garden, wheelbarrows and carts should be selected on the basis of size and maneuverability. Choose a barrow or cart that you can handle when fully loaded without requiring medical attention when you are through. The new lightweight metal units are good for almost all garden jobs. Keep in mind also that it is better to make a second trip for the other half of the load, than to make one to the doctor. One important pointer to keep in mind when buying a cart or barrow is that the larger the wheel, the easier it is to move and maneuver. Some of the finest equipment of this type is made by The Radio Steel Company.

Hoses—Good hose, either rubber or plastic, if well cared for can last for many years. The emphasis, though, is on good hose. Cheap hose, like so many other cheap or bargain items, is not worth the effort of carrying it home. The plastic hoses available today are lightweight, durable and easily moved from place to place. Rubber hose is considered better than the plastic although it is much heavier and more unwieldy. However, rubber hose will not kink like the plastic variety.

Sprinklers—There are so many on the market it is almost impossible not to get one that will be effective on your property. The trick is to read directions and ask questions so as to get the one that will do the best watering job for your needs. For the small areas, oscillating sprinklers do the job very well, but for a large piece of property, especially a large, unobstructed lawn area, select a rotating type. Of course *the* most effective watering systems are automatic underground sprinklers, discussed more fully later in this chapter.

Spraying Equipment—The war against insects, diseases and funguses may seem endless. However, with the right equipment and a regular spraying program, the war becomes a few well-spaced skirmishes.

Most insecticides, miticides and fungicides come in two forms: liquid or dusting powder (many of the powders are wettable to form a liquid spray). It is almost impossible at the outset to determine which type of chemical you will use most often. This makes the decision to buy a sprayer or a duster a difficult one. Spraying in liquid form is simpler

Plastic sprayer has large capacity but is very lightweight.

and seems to give a better idea of the amount being sprayed, while the dust, clinging to the surface of the plants, gives you a visual idea of exactly what has been protected.

The cannister or plunger type of sprayer is probably your best bet as a beginner, and should be purchased in the three-gallon size. With this type of sprayer and one of the all-purpose sprays you should be able to protect most, if not all, of your plants with a single loading. Unfortunately, when loaded, these sprayers become quite heavy, too heavy in fact for most wives to handle. If this is a consideration, several fine English sprayers, made of plastic, like the Sovereign, are perfect for the once a week spraying of roses or fruit trees by the lady of the house.

Make sure all sprayers are cleaned after use, and that toxic sprays, like weed killers and other herbicides are never used in the same sprayer as that for insecticides and other chemicals. It is wise, therefore, to have one sprayer for all non-plant killing sprays and a second for the sprays that kill or inhibit growth of vegetation.

LAWN EQUIPMENT

This is the most expensive area of maintenance equipment, requiring the purchase of a lawn mower (probably with a sweeper or grass-catcher attachment), a spreader-seeder, and possibly even a power-edger trimmer. These items can then be supplemented through local rentals with such items as thatchers, rollers and aerators.

Lawn mower—Selecting a lawn mower should be done with as much or more care than you use in selecting a family car. The comparison is not as strange as it may seem since the list of considerations in each case is long and reasonably unique to the individual buyer. Some of the things to think about when looking at mowers are:

1. Size of your property. The width of the lawn mower determines the width of the cut. The size of your property really should decide the width of the mower. For lawn areas up to and including one-fourth acre (10,000 square feet), a mower with an eighteen-inch cut is recommended. On plots of 15,000 square feet, a twenty-one-inch mower is the minimum suggested, with a twenty-four-inch mower almost a necessity for lawn areas of 20,000 square feet (one-half acre) and up.

2. Type (reel or rotary). Much can be said about the advantages of each type, but we must remember that each is really made for a specific situation. Reel-type mowers are made for use on the very finest lawns where the end result must be as close as possible to a putting green. Rotary mowers are better adapted to the greater majority of

Tractor-type mowers are a must for lawns over one half acre.

lawns where there is a bit more roughness or bumpiness in, around and under the lawn area.

3. Horsepower. Be certain the mower you buy has enough horsepower to do what is expected of it at a reasonable rate of speed. Be absolutely certain, especially with riding mowers, that the mower has enough power to go through moderately tall grass, with you on it. Keep this in mind when you don't feel like mowing the lawn. Suggest to your wife that because she's so much lighter, she'll add years to the machine's life by riding the mower herself.

4. Maneuverability. If your property now has or will have, many trees, shrubs, plantings or other obstacles, the lawn mower you choose can mean even more. The large mowers, and especially the riding mowers are quite unwieldy when it comes to maneuvering around obstacles, and may often require several trips around a single tree to do what a smaller mower can do in a single pass. And, the riding mower may not do it as well. Be sure also that you can handle the mower before you buy it. The idea is for you to guide it, not to chase it around the lawn.

5. Self-propelled or Push Type. Small, light reel mowers are generally of the push type. However, for rotaries over twenty-inches wide, self propulsion becomes a necessity. The weight of the mower plus the

amount of area it is expected to cover precludes the selection of a push-type mower.

To summarize, select your lawn mower on the basis of the job to be done. Though it may not happen often, the chore of mowing the lawn can be a pleasure if you are using a mower that is best suited to you and your property. Consider seriously the fact that there will be times when it is just not possible for you to mow the lawn, and it may be absolutely necessary for your wife to do it. Perhaps she will even take over the job if you buy her a riding mower . . . buy it, buy it!

Combination Units—In the next few paragraphs appear several of the possible combinations which exist and which should be considered before the choice of lawn mower is made. Most of this equipment is usually handled on a rental basis, but is possible for you to own with interchangeable attachments. This latter arrangement uses a compact, detachable engine unit, or "Power-Handle," as the Toro people call it. The user can quickly switch from lawn mower to tiller to edger trimmer with merely the twist of a few nuts and bolts. Additionally, the same Power-Handle can be used to drive a sprayer, pump and in the winter, a snow blower. There is little or no loss of efficiency with these combination units and the Toro is considered one of the best, interchangeable or not. It gives the homeowner the opportunity to own some or all of the tools he might possibly need at an economically feasible price. He can also add to his collection as his jobs and his budget grow. This option should be considered before the purchase of a lawn mower or other piece of equipment is made.

Spreader-Seeder—If you ever hope to have a nice, even, well-growing lawn, eliminate hand seeding and start looking for a mechanical spreader-seeder. And, again, look for the best one made, for your lawn and your needs. Look for one that is easy to push. As with lawn mowers, the size you buy is determined by the size of your property—up to 10,000 square feet, buy an eighteen- to twenty-four-inch spreader, over 10,000 square feet, buy at least a 24-inch spreader.

Unfortunately, the very purpose of a mechanical spreader-seeder— even distribution of fertilizer and seed—has been defeated by the manufacturers. Most of them make no provision for marking the areas fertilized or seeded (lime you can see), so the job becomes vague and chancy, no better than with hand seeding. Many lawns are "striped" for just that reason. Scotts, however has a flour dispensing attachment on the side of the spreader that leaves a line as you walk along. This is not too good for your shoes, but it's terrific for the lawn. So, when making your selection, look for this marking gadget, a large capacity, and easy disassembly for cleaning.

Fertilizers contain chemicals that are highly corrosive to metal surfaces so it is important that you clean your seeder after each using to ensure good working order.

Watering Systems—There are probably as many different kinds of watering devices currently on the market as there are people to use them. Without doubt, the best system devised to date is the automatic underground sprinkling system.

These systems put the right amount of water where you want it, when you want it no matter where you are. Though many of these systems are expensive and must be installed by professionals, there are some that you can put in yourself. Obviously, if you are going to install a sprinkler system and are planning a lawn, it makes sense to put in the sprinkler system first so it can save you all of the time, effort and annoyance of keeping the grass seed moist until it germinates. It can also be installed after the lawn is in without damaging the lawn. Of the do-it-yourself systems, the Moist-O-Matic can be installed over a

Pop-up sprinklers are especially effective in flower beds.

Tillers do a fine job turning over garden soil.

weekend and is relatively inexpensive compared to other systems and as an investment over a period of years. The operation of these systems is magnificently simple—a timer activates the system at a set hour every day or better yet, every night when water pressure is highest and no one is around to get wet. The system waters one section at a time, puts out a predetermined amount of water and then turns itself off. This insures that the lawn, shrubs, flower and vegetable gardens are watered on a schedule and with an amount of water that will keep them growing beautifully even in the hottest summer weather. Also, if your property is of any size you seem to spend half your life laying out, setting up, and moving sprinklers. Should the day suddenly turn windy, you may find that you have watered your neighbors lawn for several hours. It is especially ideal for people on vacation. Many a happy family has returned from a vacation to sadly discover that their once lovely green lawn is now a not-so-lovely brown.

Other Lawn Equipment—Power-edgers, trimmers, aerators, thatchers and rototillers are not used too often and may be rented. When renting, make sure you are dealing with a reliable company and that the equipment you are getting is in A-one shape and is not a possible hazard to life and limb. For example, since a thatcher throws back (toward the operator) a considerable amount of dried grass clippings, as well as dirt, stones, etc., make sure that the one you rent has a deflecting curtain on the back to protect you.

Snow Blowers—It may seem incongruous to list snow blowers as part of lawn equipment, but there are several good reasons for doing so. First, salt used to melt ice and snow will damage any lawn area with which it comes in contact. Shoveling often results in slicing the edges of the lawn along walks and driveways. Besides, a snow blower is a worthwhile investment because of the tremendous exertion involved in clearing a long, long driveway of wet, heavy snow.

CARE AND MAINTENANCE

All gardeners should learn to clean their garden tools and put them away immediately after using them. Care is a considerable part of the secret of tool and equipment longevity.

Hand tools—Ideally, all hand tools should be cleaned after every use. Remove all soil from shovels, rakes and hoes while it is still fresh and before it has a chance to become hard and crusted. Don't use a trowel or other metal tool to knock or scrape dirt from spades, hoes or other tools. Metal scraping against metal, scratches and roughens the blade's surface making the tool harder to use and more susceptible to rust. Use a hard plastic scraper or wooden spoon. Water may be used to wash mud and dirt from metal blades. If so, wipe carefully with a dry rag after washing and then again with an oily rag to inhibit rust.

Preparing hand tools for winter requires very little effort if the tools have been maintained throughout the gardening season. Simply clean, wipe dry and wipe again, with an oil or grease soaked rag and put the tools away in as dry a place as possible. Any rust that may have appeared on blades or metal parts should be removed with steel wool before storage.

If any of your tools, such as hedge clippers, garden shears, etc., need sharpening, have this done before you put them away for the winter.

Ideal way to keep tools near at hand is in specially built shed.

When they are put away sharpened, they are ready to be used in the spring when you want them.

Hoses—There is very little care and maintenance required to keep plastic or rubber hose in top shape. One good idea is to put the hose away after each use. If it is left lying about, day after day in the hot sun, it will dry out and crack. That's one of the advantages of the walking sprinklers—they wind themselves up and all you need do is put the entire unit into the garage or shed overnight. Similarly, hoses should not be left out over the winter. Pick them up, drain out all the water (so it will not freeze) and put them away until they are needed again in the spring.

Lawn Mowers—There are few homeowners who invest in more expensive machinery than their lawn mowers, but there are too many homeowners whose lack of care for this equipment leads to costly repairs and even replacement after a very short time. Normal care and maintenance of a lawn mower is neither difficult nor dirty, provided it is done after each mowing, especially after mowing when the grass is a bit wet.

Check the handbook provided by the manufacturer of your lawn mower and clean it according to his step-by-step instructions. Be sure the mower is completely disconnected and cannot possibly start accidentally before putting your hands near the blade. This is usually accomplished by disconnecting the spark plug or ignition wire. Clean out all grass clippings, soil and twigs and check to be certain nothing has become wrapped around the blade shaft or wheel axles. Wipe off the entire mower and give metal parts a once over with an oily rag.

With this routine but important maintenance completed after each use, the special steps required for winter protection are minimal. After the last mowing of the season, clean and wipe as indicated. Remove the oil filter, clean and replace it. Run the engine until it runs out of gas. (The mower should never be put away for the winter with any gas in the tank.) Drain the old oil out of the crankcase and refill with fresh clean oil. If your equipment manual indicates any other protective measures, do them. Otherwise—that's it.

CHAPTER 3

Soil Conditioning

Something will grow everywhere, but not everything will grow everywhere. So, take heart. No matter what kind of soil surrounds your house, something will grow—and not only weeds. If soil problems and problem soil were insurmountable, many private homes would be creatively landscaped with the pick of the weed crop.

Among the many things you cannot control when buying a new house, is the kind of soil around it. This may even be an advantage because so few people know what to ask for. To make matters worse, the builder has left what he calls topsoil, covering every kind of trash and debris imaginable. To further compound the crime, he has also managed to reverse the position of subsoil and natural topsoil, he has compacted the soil with heavy equipment, he has left hills and valleys, lumps and clods, and he has done such a good job of disrupting nature's balance, it appears that nothing will ever grow.

It is here that nature, in all her majesty, and the homeowner, with all his ingenuity, team up to produce the flowers, grass, trees, shrubs and even vegetables that help make a house a home.

Once over the urge to do bodily damage to the builder and his motley crew, the next step is to analyze the available soil with an eye toward what you want to grow in it. On farms or other large acreage being prepared for initial planting, the process involved in determining the kind of soil available is scientific, lengthy and extremely detailed. For the new homeowner, this same process can be compressed into a few basic steps: finding out the type of soil, testing it and rehabilitating it.

SOIL TYPES

The most important factor in determining good or poor soil is its structure. Soil structure determines the amount of water and nutrients retained and passed on to plant roots, the amount of compaction and thus, the amount of difficulty a newly germinating seedling has in pushing to the surface. It also determines the amount of time required for the soil to dry out and warm up for spring planting, the ease or difficulty with which you dig into and work the soil and, of course, just what must be added and how much, so you can plant and grow the things of your choice.

Since soil is broken into three distinct groups, each with characteristics that become readily apparent upon examination, it is important for the new gardener to be able to recognize each group, know the basic pros and cons of each, and what can be done to bring any of the types to where it grows specific plants.

Loamy Soil—If you have loamy soil, you are in good shape, because this is the kind of soil everyone works to get. Made up of the other two types of soil, clay and sandy, but mixed with plenty of humus, loamy soil holds just the right amount of water and plant nutrients, is neither too light nor too heavy, and is a fine medium for the multiplication of bacteria that help keep plants healthy and well-fed. If this is the kind of soil you have, be grateful, and get right on to planting. If not, read further.

Sandy Soil—Sandy soils are quite light, but not lacking in all other attributes. They are not quite as bad as clay soils, since they require considerably less effort to bring up to par. Quick to warm up in the spring and quite easy to work, this type of soil must be fed frequently because the nutrients leach through and out, giving food to the plant's roots only on the way through. Adding large amounts of organic material such as peat moss, compost and humus will bring sandy soils into the loamy or ideal category. If your soil is sandy, don't be afraid to add, add, add organic matter.

Clay Soil—If your soil is heavy and claylike, you have your work cut out for you. Because of their heavy texture, clay soils retain vast amounts of water. As a result, they do not dry out as quickly as is desirable in the spring and also tend to form hard crusts when they do finally dry out. To help eliminate a clay condition, the soil must be loosened, aerated and treated with additives to help it drain. Add humus, sand and compost in large quantities and mix well, preferably with a tiller implement. If at all possible, plow up clay soils the season before planting, and allow large clods to remain on the surface. The effect of sun and wind combined with the alternate freezing and thawing common in winter does much to alter the texture of the soil.

The soil types described here are all extreme conditions, and the new gardener should be aware that variations of the three are prevalent. The idea is to find what your soil problem is and treat it accordingly.

SOIL TESTING

A soil test tells you what's in your soil in the way of acids and fertilizer components. Then, knowing what is in the soil, you can find out what it needs.

Soil testing should be carried out as scientifically as possible. In most areas a state or county agent will test your soil and give you an analysis, reducing your part in the exploration to the collection of soil samples. However, even the task of collecting the samples, requires care, if the results are to be accurate and worthwhile.

Because the idea of the soil test is to give an average result over your entire property, samples must be taken from various parts of the property. If at all possible, do your soil testing in the fall when the soil has been through a growing season and the nutrient level is closer to normal than at other times of the year. Need more reasons for fall testing? Spring soil is usually wet soil and this can delay and complicate your testing activities. In addition, soil-testing laboratories are usually busier in spring than fall and this can delay your test results. Before you go out with spade and wheelbarrow to collect soil samples, trade in your shovel for a teaspoon and your wheelbarrow for a small envelope. All that is needed, in volume, for a good soil test is a teaspoon or two of soil.

Take small samples from at least two dozen areas on your property. Dig down about eight inches with a trowel or sharp-pointed spade. Special tools are available to do the sampling job, but the new homeowner should not concern himself with these because a trowel will do a creditable job. Bring up a small sample from eight inches down and collect in a clean paper sack, glass jar, plastic bag or other clean container. Collect a sample of about teaspoon size from each of the sample areas. Remember, it is not necessary to collect huge soil clods or to dig up half your property for a successful, accurate test.

Wet soil should be dried on clean paper at room temperature before it is mixed with the other samples preparatory to shipping out for testing. Dry soils should be mixed thoroughly and packaged for mailing. Check with the testing lab (the county agent or state agriculture experiment station) for instructions on mailing, labeling and the cost of the test. Though some testing labs have no fee, the majority do charge a small fee, generally between fifty cents and three dollars for each sample. Whatever the charge and wherever the test is done, having it done is important; the results will guide your actions in liming, fertilizing and other soil conditioning.

LIMING

Considering the miraculous way in which nature works, it is not surprising to learn that there is a soil acidity level at which each plant grows best. It is also not surprising that nature has allowed for a multitude of variables and endowed plants with the ability to grow well in a reasonably wide range of soil conditions. Because it is easy to regulate the acidity level of soil, there is no reason why new homeowners should not strive for the very best.

Liming, or adding limestone to the soil, will lower the acidity level, according to the amount used, to a point at which your prized plants will thrive. If a soil test indicates that your plants require soil at a different pH than the soil currently has, get ready to spread some lime.

There are three different kinds of lime available for this purpose: hydrated lime, ground lime and dolomitic lime. Because lime is relatively inexpensive, and the price differential between the three types is of such little consequence, the new gardener should lime with dolomitic lime; it does more for you. Along with its neutralizing abilities, dolomitic limestone adds calcium and magnesium to the soil, further enhancing its ability to produce. The amount of limestone to apply is best determined by the people who test your soil; they will indicate the number of pounds necessary to lower the acidic level of your soil. Follow their recommendations carefully for even though the possibility is a small one, it is conceivable that overliming may result in plant damage.

Apply the lime in the fall and work it into the soil thoroughly to a depth of about six to eight inches. Fall liming allows several months for the lime to act within the soil, and gives you enough time to know that the lime has become a part of the soil, and is working. Maintain a stable, soil acidic level by liming after each three year soil test. This will assure you of soil with an acid level at which most plants flourish.

High Alkalinity—A similar situation and solution exist where soil is too alkaline for good plant growth. By adding sulphur or aluminum sulphate to the soil at rates indicated by your soil test, the soil acidity will be increased to the recommended level. The same procedure should be followed as was indicated for liming. Don't do either job "by eye." Determine the requirements of your soil and meet them as carefully and accurately as possible.

BEST pH FOR SELECTED PLANTS*

Plant	Best pH	Plant	Best pH
Apple	5.5-7.5	Lettuce	6.0-7.0
Asparagus	6.0-7.0	Lilac	6.0-7.5
Azalea	4.5-7.0	Oak, Pin	5.0-6.5
Beans	5.5-6.5	Onions	6.0-6.7
Beets	6.0-7.5	Peach	6.0-7.5
Birch	5.0-6.5	Pear	6.0-7.5
Blueberries	5.0-5.8	Peas	6.0-7.0
Cabbage	6.0-7.0	Peppers	5.5-6.5
Carnation	6.0-7.5	Pine	4.5-5.0
Carrots	5.7-7.0	Potatoes	5.0-5.5
Cauliflower	6.0-7.5	Radishes	5.5-6.5
Cherry	6.0-7.5	Raspberry	5.5-7.0
Chrysanthemum	5.5-7.0	Rhododendron	4.5-6.0
Corn	5.5-7.0	Roses	6.0-7.5
Cucumber	5.5-6.7	Spinach	6.0-7.0
Eggplant	5.5-6.0	Spruce	5.0-6.0
Fir	6.0-7.0	Squash	5.5-6.5
Geranium	6.5-8.0	Strawberries	5.0-6.5
Gladiolus	6.0-7.5	Sycamore	6.0-7.5
Grass	5.5-7.0	Tomatoes	5.5-6.7
Hemlock	5.0-5.5	Tulip	6.0-7.0
Iris	5.0-7.0	Watermelon	5.5-6.5
Juniper	5.0-6.5	Weeping Willow	5.5-7.0
Laurel	4.5-6.0	Zinnia	6.0-7.5

* (Neutral soil is indicated as a pH of 7.0. Numbers below that indicate higher acid levels (6.0 is high in acid, but 5.5 is even higher) and numbers above 7.0 indicate alkalinity in a similar fashion. Add lime to neutralize (bring 5.5 up to 7.0) and add sulphur or aluminum sulfate to make soil more acidic.)

FERTILIZING

Referred to in many different ways, fertilizer is best described as plant food. Just as humans need a balanced diet to keep healthy, with special emphasis on certain nutrients, plants also require a balanced diet, with special emphasis on three major elements—nitrogen, phosphorous and potassium. These three building blocks to good, healthy plants are removed from the soil by growing plants and must be replaced. Not only are these elements necessary for plant growth, they are also the cause for some distinction between veteran and neophyte gardeners. The old timers speak casually of 10-6-4, 5-10-5, 8-24-8, leaving the greenhorn speechless. Here's the secret of the numbers. Fertilizer is rated according to the amount of the three aforementioned elements it contains, and this rating is stated in the form of their ratio to each other (These percentages must be clearly marked, according to law on each fertilizer container, so you know what you are buying). Knowing the requirements of your plants, flowers and vegetables, and knowing what types of fertilizer are available you can select, for example, a fertilizer high in nitrogen (10-6-4) or one high in phosphorous (8-24-8). Under this system, a bag of fertilizer marked 10-6-4 contains the three elements, nitrogen-phosphorous-potassium, in that order, in a ratio of 10 pounds to 6 pounds to 4 pounds per 100 pound bag.

Organics—The wastes or by-products of plants and animals—organic fertilizers—take the form of animal manures, composted plant materials, bone meal, sewer sludge and slaughter house wastes. Though many gardeners prefer these natural materials to the chemical or inorganic fertilizers, they are best used by the beginning gardener as a soil supplement and fertilizer in combination with inorganics. Organic materials are quite bulky for the percentage of nutrients they add to the soil, so they are relatively expensive to use and difficult to measure accurately. Because organic fertilizers are insoluble, they must be mixed with the soil so they decay, releasing their nutrients to the soil and then to the plants. This process takes time, so organics make fine soil conditioners, and as fertilizers, they add a measure of nutrients to the soil, are slow acting and long lasting.

Inorganics—More commonly used than organics today, the inorganic fertilizers are made of mineral salts or chemicals to an exact analysis, and are easy to use and control. Soluble in water, the inorganic fertilizers are quickly available to plants and, for the same reason tend to leach out after considerable watering. Because they are highly concentrated, extreme care must be exercised in their use, for if these fertilizers are allowed to come in contact with any of the smaller roots of trees, shrubs, or other plants, they will burn the roots and often seriously damage the plants.

Application—There are as many ways of applying fertilizer as there are fertilizers and things to fertilize. The most important recommendation is to follow the directions on the package. Don't measure "by eye." If the package indicates that a single pound should be applied to one hundred square feet of soil or lawn, don't apply one and one-half or two pounds. Modern chemicals do not fit in with the philosophy that, "if one is good, two is better." Fertilizer applied according to directions will feed the plant and give it what it needs to grow well, an overdose may kill it.

Trees and Shrubs—Early spring is the best time to fertilize trees and shrubs so they have the nutrients necessary to make the most of the coming growing season. Fertilizing once a year is usually enough to insure good growth and healthy trees and shrubs. In especially poor soil, a feeding in very late October, after the leaves are off the trees will help the plant build a good root system. Wait until all leaves have fallen before fertilizing or new soft growth will appear and be winter killed, damaging the tree or shrub.

For best results with shrubs, spread complete fertilizer by hand over the area around the trunk. Approximately one and one-half pounds of fertilizer should be spread for a fifty square-foot soil area. Work the fertilizer into the soil, but not too deeply. Many shrubs are shallow rooted and deep cultivation can damage roots. After the fertilizer is worked into the soil, water well.

Trees are best not fertilized on the surface as this may encourage shallow root growth, weakening the trees. Instead, make holes with a crow bar and sledge hammer about fifteen to eighteen inches deep and the same distance apart all around the tree to a point past the tip of the longest branch. Pour about one-eighth pound (2 ounces) of complete fertilizer, say, 10-6-4, into each hole and water thoroughly.

Hole spacing for fertilizing large trees

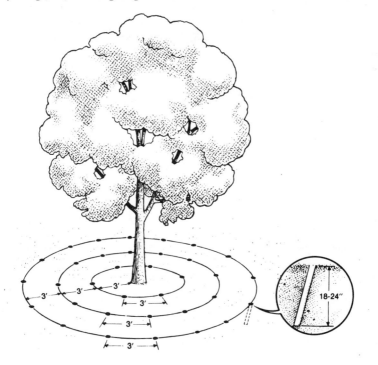

Lawns are fertilized at least three times each year and for this job a mechanical spreader is a necessity. Accuracy is extremely important, not only in the amounts of fertilizer used, but also where the fertilizer is placed. Uneven placement of fertilizer will result, in a very short time, in a striped lawn. The fertilizer must be put down in rows, one right next to the other. Spaces between rows will show up and ruin the appearance of your lawn.

Vegetables and flowers are fertilized on an almost individual basis, but certain suggestions are valid for all. The soil in which flowers and vegetables are to grow must first be prepared for these plants with

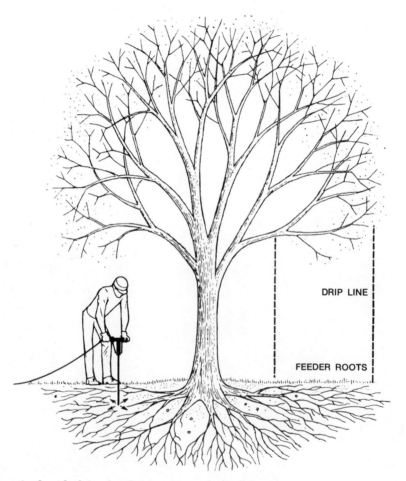

DRIP LINE

FEEDER ROOTS

Root feeder ideal for fertilizing trees and shrubs

fertilizer and other soil additives. Put fertilizer on the soil in the spring, reasonably close to the time you are going to plant. Work into the top six or eight inches and you are ready to plant.

A starter solution of fertilizer, used when transplanting seedlings, will go a long way toward insuring success. Dissolve one pound of complete fertilizer, say, 5-10-5, in one gallon of water, and then dilute this stock solution with water to make five gallons of starter solution. Vegetable plants profit from additional fertilizing just as the first vegetables are being formed. Place the fertilizer in a ring around the plant, not touching the main stem. Work in lightly and water well. Other, more detailed suggestions for vegetables and flowers can be found in Chapters 9 and 10.

SOIL CONDITIONERS

Among the most widely used and often abused materials in a gardener's repertory are the soil conditioners. These organic materials are readily available and if used properly can change your soil from unproductive concrete-like dirt to rich productive garden soil. Unfortunately, many long-time gardeners and most new gardeners bequeath large amounts of potentially wonderful soil conditioners to the garbage collectors. If they were to remember that all of nature operates on a cycle, they would realize that all garden wastes, grass clippings, vegetable wastes, corncobs, etc., should be returned to the soil to help put back some of the

Bricks around cleaned out area make trimming with mower easier

Grass and weed control chemical virtually eliminates weeding

nutrients removed by growing plants. So, before throwing out anything that grew, think a moment. There may be a better place for it than the county dump.

Mulches—One of the best ways to use garden left-overs is as mulch. The rewards are bigger and better plants and less work for you. With surprisingly little effort and often no cost, mulches do a multi-pronged job around the garden and wherever any plantings are made.

Two-inch thick mulch layer retains moisture and looks pretty

Well tended soil looks nice and grows healthy, pretty plants

First on the list of jobs that mulches accomplish is temperature stabilization. With a mulch on the ground around plants or vegetables, the soil temperature remains relatively stable, encouraging root growth and healthier plants. In the summer mulches keep the soil at a steady, cool temperature, allowing maximum growth, while in winter they maintain a cold temperature throughout, preventing alternate freezing and thawing which results in heaving plants and then damage or death to roses, shrubs and other plants.

Mulches, properly applied, play an important role in conserving the moisture level of the soil. Water that is in the soil evaporates considerably slower when the area is covered with a mulch. And, water that is added to the soil by sprinkler or through rainfall soaks in better because the soil has been kept in good condition, making it extremely receptive to irrigation. Be careful with certain mulches though, like peat moss and some grass clippings—they tend to form a barrier to water if too dry or packed too tightly.

That's not all. Mulches can almost eliminate the task of weeding in flower beds and vegetable gardens. Just about all weeds are defeated before they start because they cannot push through the thickness of the mulch. An occasional weed will come through, but it is quickly and easily pulled from the beautifully conditioned soil beneath the mulch layer.

To round out the other benefits derived from mulching, you will find that the soil is in better condition, your plants grow, bloom and bear better, fewer roots are cut by cultivation, you have less work, and last but not least, your garden or other planting areas will look better groomed.

The table in this chapter lists the most popular mulches and where and how they can best be used. Soon after planting, and the sooner the better, lay down a two- to three-inch thick layer of mulch all around the plant. Allow no thin spots or spots of soil to show through. Water the area thoroughly, both before and after putting down the mulching material. Organic mulches can be worked into the soil at the end of the growing season, adding organic material to the soil and improving its condition. If plants are diseased in any way, however, it is wise to pick up the mulch, spray the plant thoroughly, destroy the old mulch, and put down new mulch for the winter.

MULCHES FOR GARDEN AND GENERAL USE

Mulch	Comments
Aluminum Foil	Very effective as a mulch, especially around small trees and shrubs. Same foil as used in kitchen can be used for mulching. Can be covered with other materials (peat moss, pebbles, etc.) to enhance appearance.
Buckwheat Hulls	Marvelous anywhere there are plants, but especially good for ornamental plantings. Looks good, lasts long, has very good color.

Mulches For Garden and General Use *(Continued)*

Mulch	Comments
Cocoa-Bean Hulls	This by-product of the chocolate industry makes a good mulch, but does tend to become packed down. Mix with other mulches to keep loose. Dark brown color is excellent to set off roses, other flowers.
Corncobs	More readily available in Midwest than other parts of the country, corncobs do a good job, but are not as nice looking as other mulches.
Hay	Makes a good mulch for vegetable gardens and similar areas, others are better for show areas.
Lawn Clippings	Very good mulch, but shuld be left to dry out a bit before use. Green clippings right from the mower bag generate considerable heat when drying. Do not allow to mat down.
Leaves	As is, leaves are untidy and easily matted. Tree leaves make fine mulches if composted. Add extra lime to oak leaves unless used for acid-loving plants.
Manure	Makes a fine mulch when composted. Should not be used fresh because fresh manure burns. Different animal manures have different nutrient strengths. Check before using.
Marble Chips	Makes a beautiful mulch around a tree or shrub. Occasional weeds can be easily picked to keep area neat.
Peat Moss	One of the best mulches. Looks nice, has good texture. Water area before putting down as mulch, then water peat moss thoroughly once in place.
Pebbles	All sizes, shapes and colors are available and make good mulches if put down in sufficient quantity. To use fewer pebbles, put plastic film down first and cover with layer of pebbles.
Plastic Film	Excellent for vegetable gardens or other areas where performance is more important than appearance. Weeds will grow under clear plastic—none grow under black plastic.
Salt Hay	Very fine for use almost anywhere. Thin layer of peat moss on top of salt hay adds good looks to efficiency of hay as mulch.
Sawdust	Inexpensive and easily available from lumberyards or sawmills, sawdust, especially from hardwoods makes a fine mulch. Since it may cause a nitrogen deficiency, add fertilizers high in nitrogen to mulch.
Tanbark	Very good as a mulch if not allowed to pack down.

Composts—Also made from garden wastes, but adding other wastes too, compost is just about the best soil conditioner available. Called artificial manure, compost is merely vegetable or plant matter that has decomposed. Easily made by any gardener willing to save all the garden and other living wastes, this soil conditioner, once ready for use should be used generously in and around soil wherever there are plants.

To make compost, collect and save all plant and vegetable matter and pile it in some out of the way spot on your property. Enclose the area with wire fencing, cinder blocks, or other material to keep the pile neat and orderly looking. Include just about everything that once grew, such as leaves, weeds, lawn clippings, corncobs, cornstalks, straw, wood chips and vegetable garbage. Do not include paper, bones or leather as they take too long to decompose. Place the wastes on the pile in layers, and on top of each layer put a layer of garden soil and some commercial fertilizer. Fine materials such as grass clippings or straw are piled in thin layers, about one-inch thick, while coarse materials like corn stalks are piled a bit thicker. Each layer is topped with garden soil or, if available, animal manure, and watered thoroughly. Keeping the pile moist is important, for it aids in decomposition and also permits the action of the bacteria from causing extremely high temperatures.

The quicker the pile decomposes, the quicker it can be used as a soil conditioner. Use the following procedures to greatly speed up the decomposition process. Turn the pile at least once a month and water each time the pile is turned. Use fertilizers high in nitrogen to speed up the process, add nutrients to the pile, and use as much animal manure as possible on each layer of the pile.

Thoroughly decomposed compost can be used, when mixed with the soil as a conditioner, to break down clay soils and open them up so plants may receive the necessary nutrients. It can also be added to sandy soils, making them richer and better able to hold nutrients rather than allowing them to leach through with each watering. One note: add a complete fertilizer, high in nitrogen to soil treated with compost. Bacterial action depletes much of the nitrogen content of the compost and this can adversely affect your plants.

It is easy to see that compost and other soil conditioners and additives are important to your activities as a gardener. Without them you are at the mercy of the soil, whatever its condition, when you first start to garden. With them, it is quite possible to sufficiently alter the condition and composition of your soil so it will grow anything you want—grass, shrubs, trees, roses, flowers, vegetables. Use them generously, but carefully—and always as directed.

CHAPTER 4

Lawns

A lawn is to a house as a frame is to a painting. Though you will never find this equation in a mathematics textbook, it is of great importance to homeowners because you decide on the amount of time, money and effort to spend creating and maintaining a lawn. Lawns and picture frames serve the same basic purpose—both dress up, complement, and complete an otherwise unfinished picture.

GRASS AND GRASS MIXTURES

Before investing money in grass seed, invest a little time in thinking. Determine the right grass for you and your situation. Throughout the last thirty years, grass seed and grass-seed mixtures have been developed and refined to such a point that just about every homeowner has a fighting chance for a good lawn, whatever the growing environment. Consider that certain mixtures do well in full sun with a lot of watering, others need less water, while still others produce fine, green lawns in shady areas. So, selection of the right grass or grass mixture is the first important step in planning a successful lawn. Based on this premise, the table included here contains most of the information necessary to make the correct decision when you buy grass seed, sod, or sprigs.

Because no single grass is perfect for all growing conditions, seed mixtures are made up to give the homeowner the best possible chance at a successful lawn. Rarely is grass seed sold "straight," but rather is mixed with other grasses in combinations designed to do best under the average conditions prevalent in the area in which it is to be used. For example, a good seed mixture for cool, humid areas contains 50% Kentucky bluegrass or red fescue and then is filled out with other grasses to complement these major grasses. Warm, humid area grass

43

TYPES OF GRASSES

Name	Appearance	Water Needs	Sun and Light	Food Needs	Cutting Height in Inches	Area	Remarks
BLUEGRASSES							
Kentucky	Dark green, medium density	High, needs good drainage	Light shade okay	High, thrives on rich soil	1½	North and cool	Excellent in seed mixtures
Merion Kentucky	Deeper green and slightly coarser than Kentucky blue	Low	Light shade okay	High nitrogen level	1½-2	North and cool	Good for most homes
Windsor	Deep green, dense	Moderate	Light shade okay	Thrives on rich soil	1½-2	North and cool	Excellent for most homes
BENT GRASSES							
Colonial	Very fine and velvety	High	Prefers full sun	High	1-1¼	Cool	Needs much care
Creeping	Very fine	High	Light shade okay	High	¼-¾	Cool	For putting greens
Velvet	Like green velvet	Very high	Full sun or light shade	High	¼-½	Cool	For putting greens
FESCUES							
Creeping Red Pennlawn Illahee	Deep green, Fine, bristle leaved	Low, needs good drainage	Some shade okay	Moderate	1½-2	Cool	Resistant to traffic, good for play areas
Chewings	Fine, wiry and bunchy	Low	Some shade okay	Moderate	1½-2	Cool	Non-creeping, above preferred

44

Types of Grasses (Continued)

Name	Appearance	Water Needs	Sun and Light	Food Needs	Cutting Height in Inches	Area	Remarks
Tall	Coarse	Low	Some shade okay	Moderate	1½-3	Cool	Not for lawns, good for athletic & play areas
Rough Bluegrass Poa Trivialis	Light green, medium dense	High, lives with poor drainage	No open sun	High	1½-2	Cool	Good in mixtures for shady areas, lasts only few years
Ryegrass	Coarse	High	Some shade okay	High	1½-2	Most	Temporary, often more trouble than it is worth
Redtop	Coarse	Moderate	Some shade okay	Moderate	1-2	Cool	Temporary, good in mixture as nurse grass
Zoysia Meyer	Dense, resembles Kentucky blue	Low	Full sun	High	½-¾	South some moderate North	Loses all green color at first frost, regains very late spring
Bermuda	Finely textured, turns brown in winter	Moderate	No shade	High	¼-½	South and Southwest	Can become pest moving into flower beds etc.
Buffalo	Dense, grey-green	Low	Withstands extremes	Moderate	Little mowing	West and very dry areas	Good for western lawns if cared for
St. Augustine	Deep green coarse	High	Sun or shade	Moderate	Little mowing	Frost free areas	Not for heavy traffic areas

seed mixtures are dominated by zoysia, St. Augustine and Bermuda grass, while those for dry areas of the Great Plains include major portions of buffalo grass.

Be aware of your choice and select the best for both your area and your pocketbook, then you will be sure you are getting the best for your money. Most states require accurate labeling of grass seed containers with the percentages of seed types as well as filler and weed seed. Do not buy by fancy names or by price—buy the mixture that will grow best for you. A few extra pennies spent on good seed (usually containing a higher percentage of the preferred strain) at the beginning may save you many dollars later. Here, with seed, sod or sprigs, as well as all other nursery purchases, your best bet is to deal with a well-known, reliable, local nurseryman. Ask his opinion and take his advice. He wants you to come back, but not with murder in your eye.

STARTING NEW LAWNS

Once you have decided on the kind of lawn you would like, can afford and are willing to maintain, the next step is to choose the method of installation—sod, sprig, or seed. All have advantages and disadvantages, most of which fall in the areas of time and money.

Sodding—Whether to start a new lawn with seed or with sod is quickly and easily settled by answering a few questions. How much do you have to spend on a new lawn? How quickly do you want a fully established lawn? What size is your property? Is sod just about the only way to get a lawn on your property?

Sod lawns are "instant grass'—from leveled, smoothed dirt to beautiful, lush green lawn in a matter of hours. However, as with "instant" anything, instant sod lawns are relatively expensive. For example, seeding with 100% Windsor seed cost about $9.00 for 2500 square feet (there are 10,000 square feet in one-fourth acre). The same area covered with good quality sod would cost eight or ten cents per square foot or $200 to $250. Neither of these costs includes labor.

Because of this high cost, the use of premium quality sod is considered for new lawns only if money is no object, a complete lawn is needed immediately, or the property is sloped and/or terraced in such a way that it causes the seed to be washed away.

Preparation of the soil for sodding is the same as for seeding, and this is fully discussed later in this chapter. Sod is supplied by nurseries in strips, usually one-foot wide and one-inch thick, with length varying according to the equipment available to the nurseryman. To sod, lay the strips of sod on the smoothed dirt in much the same manner as you would building bricks, that is, with the joints alternating. Fit the pieces as tightly together as possible. To avoid having the sod shift as you lay it, press the strips tightly one against the other, and drive an occasional wooden peg through the sod into the ground. Pegging the sod, while helpful and convenient when working on a flat surface, is an absolute necessity on slopes or terraces. Another helpful hint for sodding use a kneeling board to prevent your heavy footmarks from marring the carefully prepared seedbed.

After you have positioned the first section of sod, put the wide kneeling board on the strip of sod. Use this board and move it along as you move forward.

After all the sod has been laid, tamp gently with hand tamper or roller so good contact is achieved between the seedbed and the sod. A small amount of good topsoil should be spread between the cracks in the sod, but only where necessary. Work the soil into the cracks with a stick or broom or rake handle. Water the sod well, and keep it moist for at least two weeks, or until the sod has become established into a solid lawn.

Sprigging—Several grass varieties, especially those that thrive in the South, are not generally available in seed form. These grasses, including Bermuda, St. Augustine, zoysia, creeping and velvet bentgrasses, must be planted as established plants in the form of sprigs or plugs. These sprigs or plugs are actually small pieces of the grass plant placed into the ground much as you would other living plants. Sprigs are individual plants or stems, and plugs are biscuit-shaped pieces of sod.

Sprigs are planted about one foot apart in checkerboard fashion with each of the live plants set into the ground and watered until well established. For very large areas to be sprigged, a shallow cut can be made with a hoe point, the plants spaced out, and then covered with soil and watered well. The leafy end of the sprig should remain above ground, and all sprigs tamped firmly into position by walking on them or by rolling the entire area.

Plugs are similarly planted, by using a special plugging tool or trowel to make the holes into which the plugs are dropped. Though plugs are a bit hardier than the sprigs and require less attention and watering, they too should be watered well after planting and kept as moist as possible until they are well established.

Preparing the Soil—Soil preparation for a new lawn is as vital as a foundation for a new house. Poor efforts in either case will result in disaster. Present homeowners should consider themselves very lucky if the builder moved the topsoil to one side while he excavated and graded. Those going into a new house, should try to have this done. These fortunate people need only replace the topsoil and then they are about ready to seed.

Since these "fortunates" are the exception, rather than the rule, a bit more detail is required concerning soil preparation for a new lawn.

First, clear all the debris from the soil. Don't allow the builder to "plow it under" in the hope it will disappear. It won't.

Check the grade of your property, that is, the slope of the land. It should slope gently away from the house on all sides. Check to make sure there are no low spots where water will collect. If much grading must be done, call in a professional, this is not a job for a man with a rake and good intentions. So you will sound like you know what you are talking about, the property should be graded between one and two inches every fifty feet.

Once the property is graded, the lucky ones may replace the topsoil and the less fortunates must either buy topsoil, fix what they have, or be content to gripe about their terrible soil. When buying topsoil, do not be taken in by appearance. Very often, that "good black earth" passed off as high quality topsoil, is nothing more than soil excavated from a lot or building site, is probably loaded with weed seed and debris and has very few of the qualities of good topsoil. Buy only

Turn over soil with fork

Rake until surface is smooth

from a reliable nurseryman or take a sample of the soil you are considering buying to your county agent for analysis and inspection.

Your county agent or state agricultural experiment station will also be able to tell you the conditioners to add to your soil, the acidity level and how to raise or lower it, and the kind and amount of fertilizer to be added to your soil. Small soil samples, taken from various spots on your property can be analyzed by your agent, saving you considerable time, money and disappointment, not only when planting a new lawn, but when planning and planting trees, flowers, and shrubs as well.

If you cannot have your soil analyzed by your county agent, certain minimum additions can be made to upgrade your soil. Once you admit that your top four to six inches of soil is not really good topsoil, start adding organic matter. These additives can be in the form of well rotted manure or sawdust, peat moss, sewage sludge, or other locally abundant organic materials like corncobs, leaves or grass clippings. The organic materials should be added to the soil, mixed in thoroughly, and made part of the soil by using a disc tractor or powerful rototiller. You can either rent this equipment by the day or can call in a contractor to do the job.

Along with the organic matter, the addition of lime and super-phosphate will also improve many soils. Untested soil from areas east of the Mississippi River usually require about 75 pounds of dolomitic ground limestone and 40 pounds of superphosphate per one thousand square feet. The organic matter, lime and superphosphate should be worked into the top four to six inches of soil after all grading has been completed.

After these conditioning ingredients have been added and mixed well, double check the grading, and be sure no low spots remain. The best seedbed for germinating grass seed is firm; neither too heavy nor too fluffy. Rake the area lightly several times to settle the soil. Step on the newly-raked soil. If your footprint sinks into the ground more than one-half inch, the soil is too fluffy for a good seedbed, so roll lightly with a medium weight roller.

Use spreader to put down fertilizer

Then put down grass seed

Immediately before the last raking, a good complete fertilizer is spread on the soil—twenty-five pounds of 10-10-10 or 10-6-4 to each one thousand square feet (that's about 250 to 300 pounds per one-fourth acre).

Seeding—The best time to sow lawn grasses is late August through early September. This does not mean it is the only time, but it is the time when your chances of success are the greatest. At this time, just about all quality lawn grasses find the cool, moist weather of early autumn perfect for germination. If however, you cannot possibly manage to spread the seed at this time, your next best bet is very early spring. Spring or summer sowing is suitable only for temporary lawns and grasses (these are plowed under as green manure before permanent grass is sown).

Since the whole idea of sowing grass seed is to cover an area with an *even* amount of seed, mechanical rolling seeders, or spreaders, are almost mandatory. Check the seed package for the correct setting for your spreader and distribute the seed carefully over the entire lawn area to be seeded. To be sure of even distribution and complete coverage, divide the seed in half and spread the first half over the entire lawn, using a spreader setting one-half that recommended. Then, take the second half and, using the same setting, walk at right angles to your original pattern. For example, walk north and south the first time, and east and west the second.

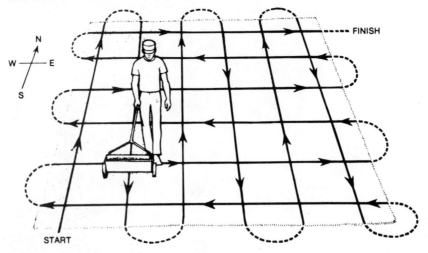

Pattern for seed and fertilizer

Seed quantities differ according to the mixture, but most of the quality seed available should be spread according to the following table:

Grass Seed	Requirement in Pounds per Quarter Acre (10,000 Square Feet)
Kentucky Bluegrass	30
Merion Kentucky Bluegrass	15-20
Colonial Bentgrass	10-20
Red Fescue	35-50
Tall Fescue	50-60
Poa Trivialis	25-30
Bermuda	10-15
Buffalo	10-15

As soon as possible after the seed has been sown, rake the entire area lightly with a spring-toothed rake. This raking should be slow and deliberate, covering the seed with no more than one-eighth to one-fourth inch of soil. Roll the entire area with a light roller to bring the seed into direct contact with the soil. Water the seeded area lightly but often until full germination has been achieved. Too heavy watering will wash away seed and also form a crust on the soil that the seeds cannot break through. Too little watering will inhibit or prevent proper growth. Water often, (two or three times each day) and lightly, increasing the amount of water slightly as the grass plants grow larger.

A good idea, sort of an insurance policy, when starting a new lawn, is to mulch the newly seeded area immediately after the first good watering. Apply a very light covering of straw or hay over the entire area and water well. Do not put down so much mulch that a mat is formed preventing the seed from germinating. A good idea is to spread the mulch lightly enough so you can see about half the seedbed

Water several times each day until seed sprouts

through the mulch. When the grass has germinated and seedlings are at least a half-inch long, carefully remove the mulch.

Start mowing the new lawn when the grass has reached the recommended mowing height for the particular variety. Do not allow the grass to grow too far beyond this height before the first mowing and between successive mowings or growth will be inhibited. Conversely, do not scalp the grass by mowing too short or the root system will not be as vigorous as desired.

TEMPORARY LAWNS

Temporary lawns are for those homeowners who want some kind of lawn (for appearance sake and to keep from being surrounded by a sea of mud during spring rains) but have moved into a new home too late in the spring to put down a permanent lawn. In this case, temporary means for a short time, not cheap as opposed to expensive. Many of the cheap seed mixtures will continue to set seed beyond the time you want them to, and this type of seed will come back to plague you, as weeds, when your permanent lawn is growing.

The best way to arrive at a quick lawn is to take your time. Condition the soil as you would just prior to seeding with a permanent-type grass seed. After conditioning, sow a common or perennial ryegrass seed and water well. The ryegrass will produce a coarse, tufty green grass that will do well until you are ready to plant a permanent lawn in late August. At this time, the ryegrass must be plowed under, the soil smoothed, and all other preparatory steps repeated. The plowed under grass adds organic matter to your soil but, more important, it allows you to put in a good lawn with a minimum of weeds after having a green cover all summer.

WEED-FREE LAWNS

A relatively new chemical, calcium cyanamide, can bring reality to the homeowner's dream of a weed-free lawn. The catch? The chemical must be used *exactly* as indicated on the package or in the short description given here.

Calcium cyanamide does two separate jobs. First, the chemical kills all weed seeds and grass and then it breaks down to form nutrients to help nourish the grass seed sown later. But, since the chemical can kill plant growth, the smallest deviation from instructions can lead to disaster.

For this wondrous weed-free lawn, go through all the soil preparation steps outlined for a new lawn, but start them a month earlier and halt the sequence just before seeding. Grade the area, spread lime and fertilizer, smooth it all out and then spread the calcium cyanamide at the rate of 225 pounds per quarter acre. Be careful that the cyanamide does not come in contact with, or even near, any trees or shrubs that you do not want killed. Keep the chemical at least *two feet* away from the roots of all trees and shrubs. If you use a lawn spreader, make sure it is thoroughly cleaned before it is put away and certainly before you use the spreader for grass seed. Work the cyanamide very lightly into the soil with a rake and water very well. For three weeks do nothing but keep the area moist.

After three weeks rake the area lightly and spread the grass seed. Water, mulch and await your weed-free lawn. It really works, but as mentioned, follow the instructions to the letter or irreparable damage can be done.

KEEPING A GOOD LAWN GOOD

Established, good-looking lawns will not remain that way long without care. As usual, care in this case, does not mean a grudging, once-a-week mowing and an occasional watering, but really means the faithful, well-regulated performance of several major and many minor maintenance activities including fertilizing, liming, weed, disease and bug proofing, watering, mowing, aerating, thatching, etc. Though the list may start you thinking about that apartment in the city again, don't worry because the various activities follow each other in sequence and are done, for the most part, only once or twice a year.

Fertilizing—Probably the most important part of lawn maintenance is fertilization. Without it, the deep green grass would soon lose its color and vigor and start to die, followed by the rapid apearance of all sorts of weeds. Therefore, lawns should be fertilized twice each season, ideally three times. The best time to spread fertilizer is when the grass is most active and making its greatest growth. The cool season grasses (bluegrasses, fescues, and bents) grow most in spring and fall and should be fertilized then. Grasses such as Bermuda grass, St. Augustine and zoysia are warm season grasses, making their greatest growth during the hot summer, so this is the time to give them additional feeding.

Fertilizer is applied to an existing lawn the same way it is to soil being prepared to accept seed. Use a reliable mechanical spreader and check the directions and spreader setting on the fertilizer bag before laying down any of the plant food.

Because both grass growth and the healthy green color are a result of nourishment provided mainly by the nitrogen in fertilizer, it is very important that sufficient amounts of nitrogen, along with other plant food elements, are introduced into the soil through organic or inorganic fertilizers.

Organic fertilizers are safer, slower and more expensive to use. However, they rarely burn the grass and are not used up as quickly.

Inorganic fertilizers are chemical compositions that are quick and easy to use, and relatively inexpensive. Over fertilization can cause grass burning but care during application will avoid this.

Unfertilized versus fertilized lawn

The nitrogen content of all fertilizers is listed first on the bag and refers to the percentage of nitrogen and its ratio to the other elements contained in the bag (a complete fertilizer contains all three major fertilizer elements: nitrogen, phosphorous, and potassium). The amount of nitrogen required by your lawn indicates the grade of fertilizer to buy.

When fertilizing a lawn, it is best to use a spreader with a marker. The marker indicates what has been covered with each pass of the spreader. Never spread inorganic fertilizer when the grass is wet. The fertilizer that sticks to the wet blades of grass burns them. Spread fertilizer on a cool, dry day. Afterward water thoroughly to wash any fertilizer off the leaves and also to start the fertilizer working.

Liming—A soil test will indicate whether or not you need add lime to your soil. Most permanent grasses do best in a slightly acid soil, (pH between 6.0 and 7.0) so judge your soil test accordingly. For "normal" soil, add lime once every three years at a rate of between 50 to 80 pounds of ground dolomitic lime for each one thousand square feet of lawn. Liming can be done at any time of the year, but is most effective in late fall or early winter when alternate freezing and thawing permits the lime to work down deep into the soil.

Watering—Improper watering can easily ruin a good lawn. Water thoroughly and water regularly. It is untrue that a little watering, several times a week is effective. Because grass roots tend to grow toward the source of water, frequent shallow watering will cause the roots to remain near the surface resulting in weak plants.

Watering is ideal with an underground sprinkler system which automatically waters the entire lawn at certain times with predetermined amounts of water. Some of the most popular underground systems for "do-it-yourselfers" can be installed all at one or a little at a time, as your budget allows. This is an especially worthwhile consideration for you when putting in a new lawn. There are a great variety of aboveground sprinklers to choose from and most are excellent. To assure that a proper amount of moisture is being absorbed into the soil, place several empty tin cans within the watering area while you water. One inch of water in a can may take several hours of watering, but this will assure you of penetration to about six inches.

Underground sprinkler head installed in lawn

Water intelligently. Water regularly, but not so long that puddles remain in spots. Do not wait until the lawn begins to turn brown before watering. Heavy soils require less frequent but greater watering than do sandy soils through which the water moves more freely. Surprisingly, a heavy downpour yields little water, so don't over-estimate the value of a rainstorm as far as your lawn is concerned.

Mowing—Keep the grass clipped regularly and at the height prescribed for your specific kind of grass. Remove only a small amount of grass at each cutting so the growth cycle of the grass is not hampered. Allowing the grass to grow very long and then clipping it results in shock to the grass plants and produces a poor lawn.

The type of mower you use depends on the kind of grass you have and the area to be mowed. Small areas may be mowed with a reel-type

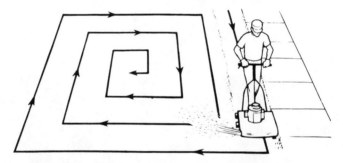

Best pattern to follow when mowing lawn with power mower

hand mower, while larger areas should be mowed with power equipment, either real or rotary. Keep the mower blades sharp so the grass is cut cleanly and not torn by the cutting edge. Remove most of the grass clippings from the lawn after each mowing; do not allow them to become matted. Matted clippings can smother the grass plants turning them brown and unsightly. Mow the lawn only when the grass is dry. Wet grass is more difficult to mow and often mats and clogs the mower. If possible water thoroughly *after* each mowing.

Aerating—This is a once every few years job that is best done with a piece of rented equipment designed to loosen extremely heavy, tight soils so water and air can get through. Holes are actually punched in the soil so nutrients, air and water may enter to condition the soil making it more conducive to the growth of healthy grass. Most lawns do not require aerating, but if yours seems very heavy and tight, check with local gardeners to see if aerating will help solve the problem.

Thatching—Lawns that require thatching are easy to spot since the thatch is everywhere to be seen, between the blades of grass on the surface of the soil. Power thatching equipment is most practically rented since the job need be done once a year, at most. The thatcher is actually a rotating power rake that scratches the surface loosening the matted grass and tossing it back toward you to be collected and removed from the surface of the lawn.

DOCTORING ESTABLISHED LAWNS

Well established, beautiful lawns often develop bald or bare spots for no apparent reason, but actually the list of reasons is long and varied. Included in this list are: lack of fertilizer, fertilizer burning, excessive wear, uneven watering, overly compacted soil, diseases, insects and a certain measure of neglect.

Determining and eliminating these causes should be your first concern as you start out to repair the spots. This can only be achieved by returning to the carefully planned lawn maintenance program outlined earlier in this chapter. Then, the bare spots can be repaired by spot sodding and spot seeding.

Spot Sodding—This is probably the easiest, fastest and all around best way to repair small bare spots. Simply take out the bad area and replace with new, healthy sod.

Remove all the dead grass and old soil from the bare area and refill the hole with good topsoil. Cut a piece of healthy sod from an area where it will not be missed (near a flower bed or back fence) and place into the bare spot. When cutting the sod, use an edger to cut through the turf. Then, using a flat-edged shovel, push horizontally about 1″ into the soil to carefully lift the sod. Once the rectangle of sod has been removed, use a knife to cut it to the shape of the area to be repaired. Place the sod into the prepared soil, tamp gently to unite the soil and the sod, and water the area thoroughly. Reseed the area from which you took the sod.

Spot Seeding—For areas larger than those that can be fixed by spot sodding, spot seeding is the answer. This system requires a bit more work and takes longer to see results, but is most economical for large bare areas.

Rake the area to be reseeded, to remove any debris, matted or dead grass. Spread a complete fertilizer and lime as required. Mix the fertilizer and lime into the loosened soil and spread evenly over the entire area. Using your mechanical spreader for large areas, and strewing the seed by hand in small areas, distribute the seed over the prepared seedbed.

Rake the area again, this time very lightly, so the seed is covered, but not buried. If a roller is available, use it to tamp down the soil so it makes direct contact with the seed. If a roller is unavailable, use a small board and step on it. Water the entire area. Water thoroughly but gently. Use the mistiest setting possible on your hose nozzle and allow the water to soak in, but not to run off. Keep the area moist until the seed germinates. Use a mulch to cover the seeded area and keep it moist while awaiting germination. Pieces of burlap, straw or fine peat moss can be used as mulch, but should be watered well before and after application to the seeded area.

Lawn Weed Control—Weeds do not grow in dense, healthy turf. So, the best way to control weeds is to keep your grass growing green and healthy. The denser the grass the slighter the chance for weeds to gain a foothold. But because few of us have weed-free lawns, the chemical companies have developed weed killers.

Crabgrass

Nimblewill

Foxtail

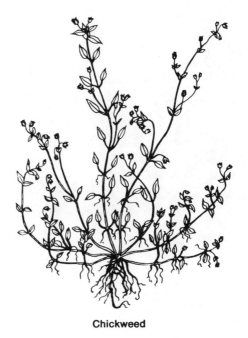

Chickweed

The current crop of herbicides is more than a match for even the wildest assortment of lawn weeds—the trick is to find out which ones you have. Identifying the weed (from pictures in the many books and pamphlets available) and finding the right chemical to kill it, (also from these pamphlets or from the local nurserymen) is fairly easy. However herbicides must be applied carefully so no other plants are killed. It is true that most herbicides are selective (killing only certain weeds), but, it is also true if too much is used or if the spray drifts, other parts of

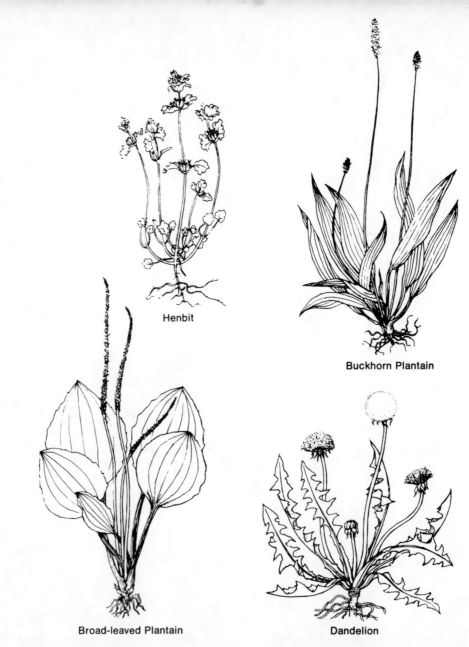

Henbit

Buckhorn Plantain

Broad-leaved Plantain

Dandelion

the lawn, or prized plants may be lost. Spray only on a calm windless day and only the amount prescribed. Get the spray nozzle as close to the weeds as possible and shield other plants from drifting spray with cardboard or other barriers. *Remember:* herbicides are poisons, and should be treated as such. Ideally, you should have a separate sprayer for herbicides. If this is not possible, wash your sprayer thorough before using it for anything else.

CHEMICAL CONTROL

Weed	2,4-D	2,4,5-T	2,4,4-TP	Remarks
Bindweed		X		
Blackmedic	X			
Buckhorn Plantain	X			All plantains
Buttercup			X	
Chickweed			X	Common & mouse ear
Cinquefoils	X			
Clover		X		
Daisies			X	
Dandelion	X			
Docks	X			
Ground Ivy			X	Spring and fall
Heal-all	X			
Henbit			X	
Knotweed		X		Get while young
Nutgrass	X			
Pennywort			X	Spring application best
Poison Ivy			X	Poison also
Puncturevine	X			
Purslane	X			
Sorrel			X	
Speedwell			X	
Spruce			X	
Thistle	X			
Wild Garlic	X			Onions also

Crabgrass control—Crabgrass, familiar to almost all gardeners and homeowners, requires special treatment. Chemical crabgrass killers comes in both pre-emergent (kills the seeding or germinating seed) and post emergent forms (kills the fully grown crabgrass plant). But because so many seeds are sent forth from each crabgrass plant it becomes virtually impossible to eliminate all crabgrass.

The best plan for crabgrass control is a systematic program carried out over a period of years designed to continually lessen the amount of crabgrass seed allowed to germinate. This kind of program cuts down considerably on the amount of seed produced. Select either pre- or post-emergent killer, whichever you prefer, and follow the instructions precisely. Continue this program over several years, while carrying out a simultaneous program to foster healthier grass growth. This combined effort should eliminate crabgrass entirely or at least keep it to a minimum.

Disease and Pest Control—Lawns, both good and bad, can fall victim to an almost endless variety of diseases and pests. Usually, the observant homeowner can spot a trouble area pretty quickly. Any unusual or different looking area should immediately be examined for worms, bugs or other insects that might feed on lawn grasses. If the cause is not obvious, take a full description and perhaps some blades of the damaged grass, to a nurseryman and he will probably be able to pinpoint the trouble. Once the cause has been determined, it is a relatively simple matter to affect the cure. After eliminating the disease or pest, make sure it does not return in that spot or another, due to faulty maintenance.

Another sneaky little hint is to keep an eye on your neighbor's lawn. The chances are good that whatever he has, you will soon have too. So, keep your eyes open and your spray gun at the ready.

CHAPTER 5

Shrubs

Few things bought by the homeowner have as many uses, and are as good a long-term investment as shrubs. Unlike most trees that normally require many years to reach maturity, shrubs are hardy growers, paying beautiful dividends a few years after their purchase.

The portfolio of special purpose and general use shrubs is crammed full of varieties of every color, shape, form and growing preference. The homeowner need only think of the specific way in which he wants to enhance his property and a wide variety of shrubs will fill the bill. As a result of the great assortment of sizes, shapes and colors as well as environmental preferences, shrubs can be used as screens for privacy, as border hedges, to mark off boundaries, as foundation plantings (both short and tall evergreens) and as specimen plantings both in the ground and in pots.

But, that's not all—shrubs can also provide all year color ranging from spring pastels and lush summer flower and berry colors to vibrant fall hues and hardy winter evergreens. The picture of versatility nears completion when we note that tall shrubs can be used as backgrounds for tall flowers and dwarf varieties can be used in rock gardens. Certain varieties can even be trained into special shapes and forms at the whim and fancy of the gardener.

SHRUB SELECTION

There are quite a lot of factors to take into consideration when trying to decide on a particular shrub for a particular spot. However, since the most important one of all is the proposed growing environment of the plant, this must be your primary consideration. It would be marvelous if we could grow anything we wanted anywhere we chose.

Obviously this is impossible, so we start to think, to select, to eliminate and finally, make a decision. Your decision must be based on some of these points; are you content to select only those shrubs which will grow in the environment you have, is the area very shady, very wet or very dry? Do you live in a city with soot, smog and little sun, or at the seashore where there are considerable amounts of sun, sand and salt spray? Or, would you like to try to change part of the growing environment to allow a wider selection of shrubs? Are you interested in improving drainage to dry out an area; fertilizing to improve the soil; planting trees for shade; or felling trees to allow sun into darkened areas?

Whatever your environmental conditions, and final decision, the variety of shrubs is large enough to permit considerable freedom of selection. It makes good sense to assume that those varieties of shrubs which are sold by local nurserymen are those which can be expected to do best in that particular area. Keep the opposite in mind when ordering by mail —the shrubs offered are grown in all different parts of the country and may not do well in your area. Choose your shrubs carefully. Keep one eye on the zone of hardiness map (see page vi) and select only those indicated as hardy for your temperature zone. From this initial group you can then select those shrubs you want for foundation planting, specimens, flowers, and other special uses you have in mind.

Foundation plantings are usually composed of evergreen shrubs, some of which flower or produce fruits besides having year-round green color.

Simple, uncluttered shrub planting makes attractive entranceway

In selecting evergreens, or any other shrubs for your foundation planting, buy with an eye on the future. Find out the mature size and shape of the plant before you buy it, and buy only those that will complement the line of your house. Just as shrubs which remain too small always look skimpy and underdeveloped, shrubs that are too large can become a problem by overshadowing a house, cutting off light and air, and even growing right up over windows or doors.

Shrub height should be varied to add interest to planting

Good general rules for foundation plantings:
1. Position shrubs so overall effect is balanced and not lopsided.
2. Use tall plants as backgrounds for flowers or shorter-growing shrubs.
3. Keep window clear by using low growers, dwarfs or varieties which improve in appearance by cutting and shaping.
4. Select plants with flower colors that go well with the color of the house.

Houses with interesting shapes require few shrubs to complete picture

5. Do not overplant. Carefully check mature height and width before planting.
6. Use only a limited number of varieties in a single area.
7. Accent building features with appropriate shrubs.

TWO DOZEN OUTSTANDING FLOWERING SHRUBS

Shrub	Flower	Blooms	Height in Feet	Area	Remarks
Abelia	Pink	June-October	7	6-10	Flowers like honeysuckle
Acacia	Yellow	February-April	25	9-10	Evergreen, rich fragrance
Andromeda	White	May	3	5-9	Lily of the valley-like flowers
Beauty Bush	Pink-yellow	June	8	5-8	Excellent background shrub
Bottlebrush	Yellow and red	April-October	20	8-10	Evergreen, dry fruits stay on all season
Buddleia	Purple and other colors	July-September	10	5-9	Lilac looking, very fragrant flowers
Camellia	Cream	Winter	25	7-10	Evergreen, white, pink, scarlet, red
Crape-Myrtle	Red and other colors	August-October	20	7-10	Great many varieties available
Deutzia	White	May-June	6	5-10	Dainty drooping branches
Forsythia	Yellow	April-May	8	5-8	Very early color, prune to keep size down
Gardenia	White	June-August	6	8-10	Evergreen in South, beautiful aroma

Two Dozen Outstanding Flowering Shrubs (*Continued*)

Shrub	Flower	Blooms	Height in Feet	Area	Remarks
Hydrangea	Purple-pink	June-July	6	6-9	Very large flower clusters
Japanese Quince	Orange	March-April	6	5-9	Beautiful big flowers
Jasmine	Yellow	July	5	7-10	Semi-evergreen, nice fragrance
Lantana	Blue-white	May-October	3	9-10	Many varieties, many colors
Lilac	Lavender	June	20	3-7	Also white, pink, some treelike
Mock-Orange	White	June	8	4-8	Very desirable shrub
Mountain Laurel	Pink	June-July	10	4-8	Also white, evergreen
Oleander	Red and other colors	June-October	15	9-10	Plant poisonous if eaten, evergreen
Shrubby Cinquefoil	Yellow-white	June-October	7	1-7	Showy clusters of flowers
Siberian Pea Tree	Yellow	June	20	1-9	Very hardy, dwarf forms too
Sorbaria	White	July-August	10	6-9	Spire-like flowers
Spice Viburnum	White	April-May	5	5-8	Nice aroma, red fall foliage
Spirea	White	May-June	3	4-8	Also pink, among prettiest shrubs

SHRUBS SELECTED FOR COLOR (*Fall Leaf Color*)

Shrub	Color	Height	Area	Deciduous or Evergreen	Remarks
Burning Bush	Red	30"	4	Both	Very diverse group
Bridal Wreath	Red	5'	5	D	White-pink flowers
Korean Barberry	Red	6'	5	D	Common as hedge
Oregon Grape	Purple	6'	5	E	Pruning keeps low
Viburnum	Purple	5'	3	D	Family has many colors
Regel's Privet	Purple	15'	5	D	Excellent for hedges
Ozark Witch-Hazel	Orange	18"	3	D	Yellow fall flowers
Fothergilla	Yellow	6"	5	D	Showy fall color
Fringetree	Yellow	28"	5	D	Showy white flowers
Leucothoë	Bronze	30"	5	E	White spring flowers

FRUIT COLOR

Shrub	Color	Height	Area	Decidu- ous or Evergreen	Remarks
Cotoneaster	Red	3'	5	Both	Pretty all year round
Cornelian Cherry	Scarlet	12'	5	D	Tart edible fruit
Japanese Beautyberry	Violet	4'	5	D	Fine for indoor arrangements
Sapphire-Berry	Blue	20'	5	D	White flower clusters
Blueberry (Low)	Blue	20"	3	D	Edible fruit
Flowering Quince	Green	6'	4	D	Good in cities too
Siberian Pea Tree	Green	24"	2	D	Very hardy
Strawberry Tree	Yellow	15'	8	E	Very slow grower
Russian Olive	Yellow	20"	2	D	Edible fruit
Wintercreeper	Orange	–	5	E	Climber
Firethorn	Orange	8'	6	E	Many uses
Rose of Sharon	Brown	12"	5	E	Grows in shade
Japanese Holly	Black	8'	4	E	Can be clipped
Silverberry	Silver red	10'	1	D	Fragrant flowers

SHRUBS FOR FOUNDATION PLANTING

Shrub	Area	Height in Feet	Shape	Deciduous or Evergreen	Remarks
Andromeda	5-9	6	stocky	E	Lily-of-the-valley flowers round topped, easy to grow
Double Almond	5-8	5	graceful	D	Many forms available covered with tiny pink flowers
Drooping Leucothoë	4-8	5	drooping low	E	Clusters of white flowers good under windows
Dwarf Japanese Yew	5-8	20	many available	E	Large, useful family, easy to grow
Dwarf Winged Euonymus	3-10	5	compact	E	Beautiful foliage, colorful berries
Firethorn	5-9	8	any	Semi-E	Very showy orange fall fruit, can be sheared
Flowering Quince	5-9	3	rounded low	D	Pretty early flowering shrub, flowers come before leaves
Garland Spirea	4-8	5	compact	D	Very free flowering with white blossoms in May
Globe Flower	5-8	6	rounded	D	Many yellow rose-like double flowers in May-June
Glossy Abelia	5-10	6	low-compact	Semi-E	Beautiful flowers, graceful growth, glossy leaves

Shrubs For Foundation Planting (Continued)

Shrub	Area	Height in Feet	Shape	Deciduous or Evergreen	Remarks
Gold Drop Bush Cinquefoil	5-8	4	low	D	Large showy white flowers in June
Japanese Holly	5-9	10	compact	E	Very decorative dark green leaves, dwarfs also available
Leather-Leaf Viburnum	5-9	10	compact	E	Striking large leaves, white flowers, red berries
Mountain Laurel	4-8	10	bushy	E	Broad-leafed favorite white, pink or rose flowers
Oak-Leaf Hydrangea	7-9	6	rounded	D	Snow ball bush, leaves look like oak
Oregon Grape	5-9	6	prune to shape	E	Leaves look like English holly, yellow flowers, April-May
Pfitzer Juniper	4-8	9	spreading pyramidal	E	Gray-green color, many varieties available
Redvein Enkianthus	4-8	10	bushy	D	Attractive yellow flowers with red in May
Slender Deutzia	5-10	6	arching branches	D	Graceful shrub, covered with white flowers in spring
Wintergreen Barberry	5-10	6	prune compact	E	Good mixed with other evergreens

73

SHRUBS FOR SEASHORE PLANTING

Shrub	Height in Feet	Area	Remarks
Bayberry	8	4-9	Semi-evergreen, berries make wax for candles
Beach Plum	6	4-8	Deciduous, has fruits with pleasant taste
Groundselbush	10	5-8	Has white fruit and flowers
Sea Buckthorn	20	4-8	Male and female required to get orange fruit
Scotch Broom	9	2-6	Flowers May-June, many varieties available
Sweetshrub	3	3-8	Fern-like leaves cover sandy areas
Sweetspire	6	5-8	Fragrant yellow flowers in June-July
Sweet Pepperbush	10	3-9	Fragrant white or pink flowers in August-September
Salt Tree	5	6-8	May-June blooms of light purple
Honeysuckle Morrow	8	4-8	Pleasant white flowers May-June

SHRUBS FOR CITY DWELLERS

Shrub	Height in Feet	Area	Remarks
Cornelian Cherry	12	5-8	Has yellow flowers March-April, tart edible fruit
Burning Bush	3	3-10	Beautiful rosy pink fall foliage
Rose of Sharon	12	5-8	Very late bloomer August-September, various colors
Oregon Grape	6	5-9	Hollylike leaves, April-May, yellow flowers

Shrubs For City Dwellers *(Continued)*

Firethorn	8	5-9	Semi-evergreen showy orange fruit in fall
Mountain Laurel	10	5-8	Evergreen large red flowers, May-June
Korean Bay	2	5-10	Foliage dark green very fragrant
Andromeda	3	5-9	Lily-of-the-Valley type flowers, May
Japanese Holly	8	5-9	Can be shaped, leaves like boxwood

HEDGES

Just about any shrub placed one beside the other can be made into a hedge. Of course, some shrubs make better hedges than others, so it depends upon what kind of shrub hedge you want. The list of hedges included here gives enough variety for anyone to be able to select a formal or informal, deciduous or evergreen hedge.

Planting shrubs to form a hedge is just the same as planting specimen plants, except that there are more of them. Instead of digging individual holes for each shrub, dig a trench about two-feet wide and space the plants according to the eventual adult mature size. Plant, water, fertilize, and maintain the same as any other shrub.

Shrubs break up extra long length of ranch-type houses

Pruning hedges is somewhat different than pruning individual shrubs, because hedges are pruned for overall effect and individual shrubs are pruned as specimen plants. Prune hedges carefully in the spring just before new growth starts and in the summer as required to keep new growth within bounds. Prune hedges so the top of the hedge is slightly narrower than the bottom. Not too much of a difference, but just enough

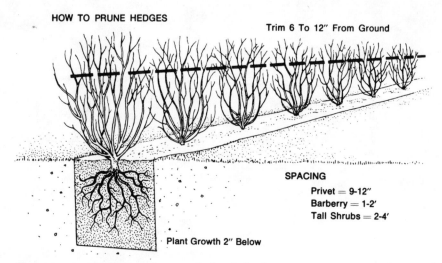

HOW TO PRUNE HEDGES

Trim 6 To 12″ From Ground

SPACING

Privet = 9-12″
Barberry = 1-2′
Tall Shrubs = 2-4′

Plant Growth 2″ Below

Correct way to plant and prune hedged shrubs

so the sun can get to the bottom of the hedge and keep it healthy too.

Don't shy away from a hedge, thinking that all hedges are privet hedges and must be carefully trimmed and manicured. There are enough varieties available so you can select one that is exactly what you want, trimmed or natural, tall or short, evergreen or deciduous, flowering or berried.

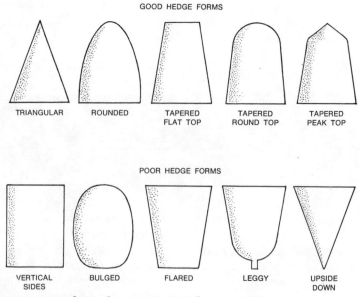

GOOD HEDGE FORMS

TRIANGULAR   ROUNDED   TAPERED FLAT TOP   TAPERED ROUND TOP   TAPERED PEAK TOP

POOR HEDGE FORMS

VERTICAL SIDES   BULGED   FLARED   LEGGY   UPSIDE DOWN

Hedges are pruned to a large variety of shapes

BEST SHRUBS FOR HEDGES

Shrub	Area	Height in Feet Sheared	Height in Feet Natural	Spacing in Feet	Deciduous or Evergreen	Remarks
Cherry Laurel	7-9	10	30	3	Evergreen	White flowers, can be sheared
Chinese Honeysuckle	6-9	2	6	1½	Evergreen	Outstanding leaves, good at seashore too
Cotoneaster	5-9	—	3	2½	Deciduous	Also good in rock gardens
Doublefile Viburnum	5-9	—	10	3	Deciduous	White flowers, then red berries turn dark blue in fall
Dwarf Boxwood	6-10	2	3	1½	Evergreen	Many boxwood last 100 years or more
Dwarf Japanese Yew	4-8	2	7	2	Evergreen	Available in many good shapes and sizes
Dwarg Mugho Pine	4-8	—	4	2	Evergreen	Make interesting different hedge or border
Dwarf Winged Euonymus	3-10	2	5	2	Deciduous	Very slow growing, beautiful fall leaf color
European Privet	5-9	3	12	1½	Deciduous	Semi-evergreen in South, most frequently used hedge shrub

Best Shrubs For Hedges (*Continued*)

Shrub	Area	Height in Feet Sheared	Height in Feet Natural	Spacing in Feet	Deciduous or Evergreen	Remarks
Glossy Abelia	5-10	—	6	3	Deciduous	White, pink honeysuckle-like flowers
Glossy Buckthorn	1-8	10	15	3	Deciduous	Good also in city, birds love berries
Hornbeam	3-9	5	10	2	Deciduous	Very dense hedge, leaves like beech
Japanese Barberry	3-10	3	6	2	Deciduous	Beautiful fall color, very common as hedge
Japanese Flowering Quince	5-9	3	8	2	Deciduous	Long red flowers, resemble rose
Japanese Holly	5-9	3	8	2	Evergreen	Leaves look like boxwood, can be sheared
Mock-orange	4-8	—	10	4	Deciduous	Very fragrant white flowers
Mountain Currant	5-8	2	7	2	Deciduous	Makes good low hedge
Regel's Privet	5-8	3	6	2	Deciduous	Branches arch nicely, very good hedge
Wintergreen Barberry	5-10	3	6	2	Evergreen	Very dense hedge, has yellow flowers, dark blue berries
Yellow Sage	9-10	—	4	2	Deciduous	Various colored flowers on same plant

AZALEAS AND RHODODENDRON

Carefully omitted from the lists and discussions in this chapter are the azaleas and rhododendrons, one of the largest, most varied and beautiful groups in all horticulture. And that, is the reason for their omission, they deserve to be treated separately.

Both azaleas and rhododendrons belong to a botanical grouping called rhododendron which contains over 3,000 named varieties with colors, shapes and sizes running the entire length of a gardener's wildest imagination. It would be futile to attempt to name varieties here, but instead, note that these shrubs have something for everyone (including some members which are evergreen and some which are deciduous) and everyone should have some of them. With reasonable care, and a little knowledge, they can be grown successfully by any homeowner.

Select azaleas and rhododendron for your home while they are in bloom so you know exactly the color you are getting. Because they are sold balled and burlapped, they can be bought and planted at most times of the year, and as long as they are not allowed to dry out, they will flourish. Put yourself in the hands of a specialist in these plants, not a general nurseryman, and you are pretty sure to get planting information, hints, tips, and beautiful shrubs that will enhance your property for many, many years.

PRE-PLANTING TREATMENT

Shrubs do not usually require a great deal of care or maintenance in return for the amount of beauty and pleasure they offer. However, they do deserve to be handled and planted correctly.

Shrubs are available bare root (no dirt, just moist peat moss packed around the roots), balled and burlapped (a ball of soil dug with the plant roots, wrapped in burlap and tied), and container grown (in tin cans, plastic or organic pots), and require pre-planting attention only if they cannot be planted very shortly after arrival.

Shrubs are best transplanted when they are dormant, in the early springtime before buds and new growth start, or during early autumn when it is cool and moist. Bare-root plants must be put into the ground early enough so they have a chance to get good root growth started either before the hot, dry summer or the cold winter. Balled-and-burlapped and container-grown plants can be transplanted over a considerably longer period, but the earlier they are planted, the more quickly they become permanently established.

Mail-order nurseries usually ship shrubs bare root, wrapped in peat moss, or sealed in plastic bags. On arrival, the packages should be opened and the plant roots checked for dryness. Soaking the roots and lower portions of the plant in a tub of water for several hours restores moisture to the plant. If you cannot plant a shrub shortly after its arrival, it is a good idea to "heal it in" until planting time. Healing in is a quick temporary planting until a permanent planting can be made. Dig a small V-shaped trench, lay the shrub roots into the trench and cover with soil. Heal in only in shaded, protected spots so sun and wind do not dry out the plants. Keep the soil and the shrubs moist with an occasional watering until they are redug and planted permanently.

Container-grown and balled-and-burlapped plants require much the same treatment if time is to elapse between the time they are bought and the time they are planted. Both should be kept in shady, wind-free nooks, moistened frequently and covered with straw or other mulch to limit moisture loss.

PLANTING TO LIVE

Most shrubs and other plants will survive if planted the lazy man's way—dig a hole, drop the plant in and cover it up. But, of course, there is a better way, and it consistently gets better results.

Place the shrub on the ground at the spot where you are going to plant it. Take a good look at the shrub and its surroundings. Try to visualize what the shrub will look like when it is mature. Mark off a circle about twice as large as the roots or root ball and start digging. If you are digging in an area that has good lawn, use a large piece of heavy paper or burlap to hold the dirt that you dig out, to keep it from

Peat moss, topsoil and well-rotted manure all thoroughly mixed in planting hole

messing up the lawn. Make separate piles of sod, topsoil and sand as it comes out of the hole. Dig the hole about twice as deep and twice as large across as the root ball or roots when spread out.

Loosen the soil in the bottom of the hole with the point of your spade and mix with several handfuls of organic material like manure or peat moss, and hold the grass sod aside when digging the hole. Put the sod in the hole with the grass facing the hole bottom. Chop and mix everything in the bottom of the planting hole and gently tamp until firm. Add some topsoil and again tamp until firm.

Bare-Root Plants—Build a small mound of topsoil in the bottom of the hole and spread the plant's roots over and all around the mound. Broken or torn roots should be cut off at this time. Check the depth of the plant—it should be the same depth, or no more than one inch deeper than when it was growing in the nursery. By laying a stick or shovel handle flat on the ground across the hole you can line it up with the soil line on the plant's stem and determine the depth.

Start refilling the hole with soil, putting the topsoil in first and the sand and subsoil last. Be sure there are no air pockets left around the roots as you fill the hole with soil. Air around the roots will dry them out and injure or kill your plant. Shake the shrub gently so soil filters around roots. If the shrub requires staking, do it before you refill the hole. In this way you can drive the stake while you can see where it is going and avoid having it tear through any of the roots.

Fill the hole with dirt and tamp often but gently so that soil fills all the areas around the roots. Continue to add soil until the hole is filled up to a level about two inches below normal ground level. This depressed saucer, surrounding the tree, should be filled with water and allowed to drain slowly into the ground. Fill the saucer at least twice, adding soil after each draining so the level of depression remains constant. Cover the area with an organic mulch, (peat moss, cocoa hulls, etc.) but be sure a saucer-shaped depression remains to catch and direct water to the roots.

A very high proportion (over 35%) of bare-root shrubs' root systems are lost in the process of transplanting. As a result, the shrub must be pruned to balance top with bottom so the reduced number of roots can feed the branches. Using sharp pruning shears, first cut out all broken or dead branches. Then, cut back the remaining branches to about two-thirds of their original length.

Balled-and-Burlapped and Container Plants—All plants sold with a ball of soil around the roots should be planted with that soil ball intact. Place balled-and-burlapped plant into the hole and carefully cut away the string holding the burlap to the ball. If the burlap can be removed without disturbing the root ball, take it out of the hole. If removing the burlap will break the root ball, stop trying. Open out the burlap and spread it flat across the bottom of the hole. It will eventually rot there and will not inhibit the growth of the shrub.

Unless container-grown plants are in peat or other organic pots, the container must be removed before planting. Tin snips will usually do a quick job on tin cans and will not, if you are very careful, disturb the root ball. Very often shrubs can be removed from tin cans and other solid containers without cutting the containers or hurting the root ball.

Wet the plant thoroughly and allow it to sit until the water soaks through and the soil is solid, but not muddy. If there are no holes in the bottom of the can, punch a few with a beer can opener. Turn the plant upside-down, with the plant between your fingers and the soil resting in your palm. A solid rap on the bottom of the can with your other hand or the flat part of a hammer should dislodge it all in one piece.

You can then continue along the steps outlined above for bare-root plants. Begin to replace the soil, putting in the topsoil first and then the sand and subsoil. However, when adding soil or tamping, be very careful not to damage the root ball.

POST-PLANTING TREATMENT

Though most shrubs require the minimum in special after-planting care, they should be watched, watered and generally treated as any other valuable possession. Unless the soil in which the shrub has been planted is naturally very wet, water the shrub thoroughly immediately after planting. Do not water again until the ground around the plant becomes very dry, or a light rain teases the plant with just a little bit of water. When watering, water throughly, so the water penetrates *all* the way down to the roots.

Winter Protection—Protecting shrubs against the ravages of winter can be worthwhile, but it will rarely keep alive a shrub not hardy enough for that section of the country. It seems rather silly, in general circumstances, to try to keep any shrub growing where it doesn't belong, when the chance for success is slight, and there are so many others available that can come through severe winters relatively unharmed.

However, some degree of winter protection can be given to many shrubs, even the most hardy. This type of intelligent "preventive protection" is not designed to keep the plant warm or to allow for the growing of plants which do not belong in your area. It is, instead, a way of protecting the plant against being damaged by snow, wind and ice, and also to keep it from drying out in the winter wind and sun.

Plants that are hardy in areas with severely cold winters and heavy snowstorms should be protected against: 1) heaving, 2) sun scald, 3) excessive moisture loss, and 4) breakage due to the weight of the snow. The tried and true method here is to build some sort of protective fence around, and perhaps even on top of, specially prized specimen and foundation plants. Strips of lath spaced around the plants and covered with burlap make a fine wind screen and prevent drifts from piling up and possibly breaking some branches. Overhead protective shields can be made of any lumber or lumber and burlap combination and should be made to look like a burlap covered table. Many large specimen shrubs have been protected in this way each winter for 25 to 50 years with no snow-caused breakage.

If a heavy snow has fallen and your plants are not protected, the snow itself will do no harm. The snow acts as an insulating material and keeps your plants in fine shape until it melts. The great danger of snow damage comes from the weight of the snow pressing down on branches, bending or twisting them and often snapping them off. Once the snow has piled up on your shrubs, the best and safest thing to do is to take a straw kitchen broom and carefully brush the snow from the branches. Don't worry about the snow around the shrubs or piled up against the sides. This snow will act as a mulch or insulation, so leave it alone—just brush the heavy snow from the branches.

Speaking of mulches, they can do an excellent job of protecting shrubs from heaving—the alternate freezing and thawing of the ground in winter that results in the shrub being lifted part way out of the soil and possibly exposing roots. Be careful, however, because a protective mulch put on a shrub too soon can cause irreparable damage or even kill a plant. Putting them down too soon maintains the soil at a warm temperature, slows down the plant's transition to dormancy and makes the plant susceptible to the first heavy frost. Also remember not to pile the mulch on so heavily that air and water cannot penetrate the soil.

Spraying plants with a plastic spray, like Wilt-Pruf is another relatively new method used to help shrubs get through the winter. The object is to limit the amount of water the plant will transpire in the winter sun and wind. A light spraying with an aerosol can of plastic spray will last several months and will disappear from the leaves, in the spring, when no longer required.

PRUNING

Despite what many new homeowners and gardeners may have assumed, pruning has a far more important purpose than cutting bushes into neat, symmetrical or odd shapes. Careful pruning at the proper time of year

Flowering shrub is pretty and hides unattractive light pole

helps keep plants healthy as well as beautiful. Using sharp pruning equipment (shears, knife, lopping shears or pruning saw), remove all dead, dying, diseased and otherwise unwanted branches. Prune off branches that criss-cross and branches growing outside the normal shape of the shrub. Then, carefully prune to maintain the normal shape

Huge, shaped shrubs can be used instead of trees for special effect

of the shrub. Remember that only on certain shrubs, that will tolerate shearing, can such tools as hedge clippers be used.

Never play barber with a shrub and give it a "flattop" or "butch" haircut. Pruning of this type will probably severely limit the blooming capabilities of the shrub, if it doesn't out and out kill it. For most

Shrubs along side of house look nice and hide concrete foundation

shrubs, the ideal time to prune is during the dormant season, specifically, very early spring, just before new growth starts. At that time you can remove all the winter-killed and dead wood and actually foster better, healthier bloom and growth. By pruning in the fall, you are removing all live growth and have no way of knowing what else may be killed off during the winter.

The exceptions to this dormant season trimming are for those shrubs which require old flower buds for new bloom, such as forsythia, mock orange and garden spirea. These shrubs should be pruned just after they have flowered, so flower buds can form and be ready to bloom in the spring. These shrubs are of the type that may be cut back to the ground (if you so desire) to rejuvenate old plants and rid them of thick, unsightly old wood.

Pruning cuts should be made parallel to the branches that remain and should be flush with the adjoining branch. Stubs of branches left on shrubs are not only unattractive but rot and greatly harm the tree. Apply tree wound "paint" (a special "paint" available at garden supply shops or nurseries) to all pruning cuts if possible. Be especially sure to coat all cuts one inch or more in diameter.

Although careful pruning improves a shrub both in appearance and health, be sure the particular shrub really needs it before you run for the tools. Too many fine shrubs have been lost through indiscriminate pruning—so think before you cut.

INSECT AND DISEASE CONTROL

Controlling insects and diseases of shrubs is neither complex nor difficult. As has been indicated before, the primary task is to identify the cause of the trouble. Once this is accomplished, (through either an advanced gardening book or your local nursery) the solution is easy to administer.

A very successful preventive measure is dormant oil spraying in the early spring, before new growth starts. Application of this spray eliminates most scale insects that wintered over on the shrub and protects it from infestation by others. Be sure the temperature is over 40° before spraying with an oil spray or the shrubs may be damaged.

Many other bugs can be controlled with 5% DDT dust including most beetles, caterpillars, slugs and leaf hoppers, and still others kept under control by regular applications of all-purpose compounds.

When using insecticides, fungicides, miticides, or any other chemicals, use extreme caution and follow the directions exactly. Very often too little does no good at all and too much can burn or otherwise injure the plant. Careful attention to *all* the details on cans and containers of garden chemicals will help keep your plants hardy.

CHAPTER 6

Trees

". . . only God can make a tree," but it is the responsibility of people to plant them, feed them, maintain them and enjoy them. Most people with an appreciation of nature's beauty think something special when they look at a tree. The homeowner though, sees all this, and then a bit more. When he thinks of a tree, he thinks of how expensive they are to buy, and how long it will take before he will get a reasonable amount of shade from it.

Before starting a detailed study of trees, start considering some of the reasons for planting them: trees are beautiful, they attract birds and sometimes squirrels, and some have flowers and edible fruit. Then, adding practicality to aesthetics, they are decorative, can be used to delineate borders, act as backgrounds, and hide areas or activities better left unseen. Then, strictly practical, each tree planted on your property adds to its dollar value, with this value climbing as the tree grows.

TREE SELECTION

Knowing what a tree will do and eventually look like are a part of intelligent tree selection. Asking and answering these questions before you choose your trees will result, more often than not, in getting the proper tree.

1. *Size* How big will the tree be when it is fully grown? Will the tree be too big or too small, too thin or too fat to fit in with your house and other trees and structures on your property?
2. *Hardiness* Is the tree suited to its environment and will it thrive and grow in the climate prevalent in your area? There are enough trees from which to choose so you can buy only hardy ones that will flourish in your climate.

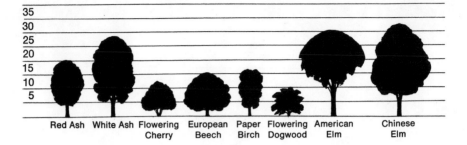

Red Ash	White Ash	Flowering Cherry	European Beech	Paper Birch	Flowering Dogwood	American Elm	Chinese Elm

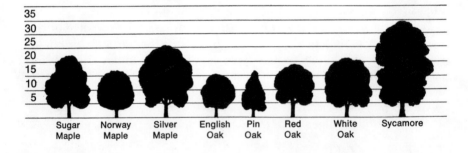

Sourgum	Ginko	Flowering Crab	Shagbark Hickory	Chinaberry	Yellow-wood	Catalpa	Weeping Willow

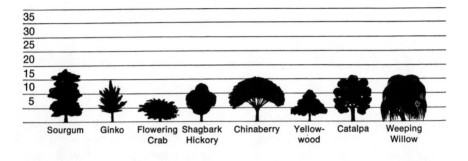

Sugar Maple	Norway Maple	Silver Maple	English Oak	Pin Oak	Red Oak	White Oak	Sycamore

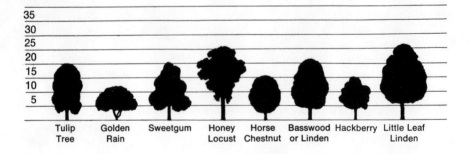

Tulip Tree	Golden Rain	Sweetgum	Honey Locust	Horse Chestnut	Basswood or Linden	Hackberry	Little Leaf Linden

3. *Shape* Trees are categorized by shape into columnar, oval, pyramidal, round, spreading and vase-shaped. Select your trees so their ultimate shape harmonizes with your house and attendant plantings.

4. *Habit* This is a matter of taste and a question of what you are looking for in a tree. From among the almost endless variety of trees available in most parts of the country, you should be able to select from trees that bear fruit, flower, give dense shade, have pretty leaves, beautiful fall color, interesting bark patterns and other special features. Find out each tree's growth habits before you buy. This information can save you considerable annoyance later.

Even the sex of certain trees is important, for with certain varieties, the female bears messy fruit. In these cases it is wise to plant only male trees eliminating the possibility of having fruit dropping on the lawn, driveway and flower beds. Other trees flower profusely and drop petals over everything.

Features to check, under the general heading "growing habits" include: shade density (is it so dense nothing can grow underneath?), odor (is it pleasant smelling or, like trees with certain fruits, does it have a strong, disagreeable odor?), and mass (is it a good tree to grow in concert with others or is it better used as a single specimen tree?).

5. *Growth* Another personal question that should be answered is: how much of a hurry are you in to have large trees? The trees are never in a hurry, they grow calmly along while homeowners, usually young homeowners, chafe at the bit to have the trees reach maturity. Although some trees do grow relatively rapidly the best bet is to select slow-growing trees that develop fully as they grow and provide beauty all the while they are growing.

A final word of caution—bargain trees are few and far between. Go to a reliable nursery and buy strong, straight, insect- and disease-free young trees. For quickest results with these trees, quicker shade, fruit or flowers, choose trees that are either ballad and burlapped or container grown over those that are sold bare root. Bare root trees are less expensive, but take longer to get accustomed to their new home and to reestablish a good root system, causing them to take longer to grow and bloom.

Unless you really know what you are doing, do not attempt to dig out your own trees in the wild or at construction sites. You won't know what you are getting, the tree may be diseased or otherwise injured and, unless you are used to this kind of heavy manual labor, the money you save on the tree will be paid to a doctor.

Shade Trees—Shade trees grow too slowly for most people, who would like to sit in the shade cast by their newly planted tree the first year, if not the first day. But, as we all quickly learn, you can't rush nature. So, the next best thing is to accept that fact pick a good shade-making tree, plant it in a spot that will give you maximum shade where you want it during the hottest part of the day and wait.

Because most, if not all, trees will give shade, selecting shade trees for the home is usually done on the basis of how much shade a particular tree gives. When making your decision on shade trees, keep in mind that trees with a great many large leaves will give very dense shade, while trees with small leaves will give a softer, more light broken shade.

Many of the evergreen trees make good shade trees, but the fact that they are evergreens may dissuade you from using them as shade trees. In the summer when shade is desirable, evergreens provide a solid, deep shade. In the winter, however, when we need as much light as possible to get us through dreary days, the evergreens still produce dense shade. As a result, deciduous trees are preferable for shade, especially when the area to be shaded adjoins the house.

Unlike some smaller specimen trees, shade trees should be bought and planted with a root ball (balled and burlapped or in a container) and should be good-sized trees. That is, buy and plant shade trees that are ten-to-fifteen-feet tall with a trunk diameter of about two inches, as opposed to seedlings or two to three foot tall trees.

A bit overdone—you can't see the house for the trees

SELECTED SHADE TREES

Tree	Shape	Color	Height in Feet	Area	Remarks
Ash					
White	Round head	Light green	60	5-8	Pretty autumn colors
Beech					
American	Pyramid	Green	80	4-8	Very hardy, yellow leaf in fall
European	Pyramid	Green	100	5-8	Many varieties available, bronze leaf in fall
Birch					
Paper	Pyramid	Bright green	90	2-6	Make beautiful clumps of 3 or 5
Chinaberry	Round	Green	50	7-10	Umbrella-like leaves look tropical
Dogwood					
Flowering	Spreading	Dull green	40	4-9	Beautiful small tree
Golden-Rain	Rounded	Light green	40	5-9	Yellow flowers are outstanding
Hackberry					
Common	Round	Light green	80	4-9	Looks like American elm
Hickory					
Pecan	Round	Green	120	6-9	Bears famous pecan nuts but of hickory family
Shagbark	Irregular	Green	100	4-8	Good fall color, edible nuts

Selected Shade Trees (*Continued*)

Tree	Shape	Color	Height in Feet	Area	Remarks
Hornbeam					
American	Round	Green	25	3-9	Multiple trunks, red and orange leaf in fall
European	Round	Green	60	3-9	Yellow foliage in fall
Horse Chestnut	Round	Dark green	100	3-10	Beautiful flowers, fruits can get messy
Linden					
American	Rounded	Bright green	75	5-8	Heart-shaped leaves, green-white flowers
Little Leaf	Rounded	Green	60	5-8	Fragrant yellow-white flowers
Locust					
Honey	Round	Bright green	75	5-9	Truly excellent shade tree
Moraine	Round	Bright green	75	5-9	Same as honey but no thorns or pods
Maidenhair	Pyramid	Dark green	60	5-9	Plant only male trees, female fruits smell
Maple					
Norway	Round	Deep green	80	4-8	Many different shaped varieties, very dense shade
Sugar	Irregular	Bright green	100	4-8	Excellent red, or yellow fall color
Oak					
Northern Red	Pyramid	Light green	75	4-8	Fast grower, red leaves in fall
Pin	Pyramid	Light green	75	4-8	Very fine specimen tree
White	Oval	Dark green	100	3-8	Extremely majestic tree

Selected Shade Trees (*Continued*)

Tree	Shape	Color	Height in Feet	Area	Remarks
Plane Tree					
American (Sycamore)	Oval	Yellow-green	150	5-8	Large, full shade tree
London	Round	Yellow-green	100	5-8	Tan bark peels off, leaves interesting pattern
Sourwood	Pyramid	Deep green	60	5-8	Red leaves in fall, fragrant white flowers
Sweetgum	Pyramid	Deep green	100	5-8	Exceptional fall color
Tulip Tree	Oval	Light green	80	5-8	Beautiful tulip-like flower, good fall color
Willow Weeping	Rounded	Yellow-green	40	5-8	Best weeper, needs lots of water
Yellow-Wood	Rounded	Bright green	40	4-8	Has showy fragrant flowers

The very small trees or seedlings, though quite inexpensive, take much too long to provide any worthwhile amount of shade. Trees of larger size will give little shade the first year, but will give good shade after a year or two. Much larger trees are expensive and often difficult or impossible for the amateur to transplant.

Because the whole idea behind planting shade trees is to gain shade, correct planning and placement are important if maximum benefits are to be derived. It is not absolutely necessary to plant huge trees to get shade. Instead, ten or fifteen footers, planted in the right place will soon serve this purpose very well. Determine when you want your house, patio or play area shaded and plant accordingly. If morning sun is desirable in your location, plant the tree to the east of the area and about twenty feet away. Midday shade will fall directly under the tree because the sun is overhead. For afternoon shade, and this is most important, since this is usually the hottest part of the day, plant trees to the west and slightly south of the area to be shaded.

City Trees—For those of us living in or near cities, the task of growing trees becomes formidable, especially in urban areas plagued with excessive amounts of smoke, soot and polluted air. This horticultural hardship does not, however, lessen our desire to see green trees, flowers, birds and the other beauties of nature.

Instead of fighting the city environment and its specific conditions, a smarter course is to join it, that is, don't try to grow trees that are weakened and eventually killed by this air, but select those trees that will tolerate the filthy air and reduced amounts of sunlight. Included in this list of hardy city dwelling trees are the American ash, elm, gingko, horse chestnut, hackberry, linden, poplar, sycamore and willow. Other trees like the honeylocust, sourgum, sugar maple, and sweetgum will grow well in cities where the air is unpolluted.

A certain amount of special attention should be given these trees if they are to have any reasonable chance to survive. Dig extra large holes when planting and fill with good topsoil to partially compensate for the poor city soil. Water well in periods of drought, feed as required, and spray extra carefully to eliminate insects and disease from the problems besetting these trees. Watch for storm, wind or ice damage, and prune and apply tree wound paint as required. Your reward, the sight of your trees flourishing in the drab city is well worth this extra effort.

Flowering Trees—When we think of flowering trees, we generally picture spring, with a magnificent show of beautiful blooms on a graceful tree. If we think it through a little further, however, we will see much more for though flowers are an almost unbeatable asset, there are other assets and reasons for planting flowering trees.

If we check the available trees and our property is large enough to accommodate several flowering varieties, we can select trees that will bloom in sequence from early spring through summer and into early fall. As an added attraction these trees will also give a gentle, clean fragrance to the air, produce fruit or berries for looking, eating or attracting birds, provide shade and endow our homes and property with beauty year round.

A word of caution—don't overdo. Small property owners are far better off with a single, beautiful flowering tree that can be seen and enjoyed in uncluttered elegance than a great number of trees that crowd each other and result in a hodge-podge of colors and forms. Plan your landscape in advance so flowering trees will be set off to advantage and justify their planting.

As with other trees and shrubs, select only those flowering trees that are hardy in your area, for it is with these that you stand your greatest chance of success. Use these trees wherever they will add the most to your overall landscape plan—in combination or backed by evergreens, as specimen trees surrounded by lawn, in gardens, or with shrubs and flowers in a small island of beauty. Remember too, that the foliage of these trees is often as beautiful as the blossoms and should be considered when selections are being made.

The list of flowering trees indicates some of the variety available to the homeowner when planning and should be used to choose the best tree for his purposes, area, and available growing environment. With so many different kinds and varieties to choose from, there should be no reason for any landscape to be barren of these beauties.

Stakes are used to help shape young trees

OUTSTANDING FLOWERING TREES

Tree	Shape	Flower	Bloom	Height in Feet	Area	Remarks
Black Locust	Round	White	June	75	4-9	Very brittle branches snap off too easily
Chinese Catalpa	Oval	Cream-purple spot	June-July	30	5-9	Huge amounts of fragrant flowers
Chinese Scholar	Round	White	August-September	50	5-8	Feathery leaves make beautiful showy tree
Dove-Tree	Thin pyramid	White	May-June	60	6-9	Large flowers look like beautiful dove's wings
Empress	Round	Violet	May	50	5-8	Looks and sometimes called purple catalpa
Epaulette	Oval	White	June	50	5-9	10-inch flower groups make beautiful display
Flowering Crabapple	Spreading	Pink, white, red	May	25	4-9	Beautiful flowers
Flowering Dogwood	Spreading	Pink, red, white	April	40	4-9	One of best and beautiful small trees
Franklin	Thin pyramid	Creamy	August-September	25	6-10	Magnificent late flowers outshine most other trees
Fringe	Round	White	May-June	25	5-10	Very showy flower display

Outstanding Flowering Trees (*Continued*)

Tree	Shape	Flower	Bloom	Height in Feet	Area	Remarks
Golden-Rain	Round	Yellow	June	40	5-9	Hardy tree, yellow flower makes this outstanding
Horse Chestnut	Round	White	May-June	85	4-10	Flowers run to 8-inch spikes, look like hyacinth
Japanese Flowering Cherry	Spreading	White	April	25	5-9	Single, double and pink flowers also available
Japanese Flowering Dogwood	Spreading	Pink, white	June	20	5-9	Very beautiful in flower and with berries
Japanese Lilac	Thin pyramid	White	June	30	4-8	Well-known beautiful bunches of flowers
Little Leaf Linden	Oval	Yellow	June-July	80	5-8	Flowers very fragrant, also called lime tree
Redbud	Round	Pink-white	April	30	5-9	Light flowers on dark bark very striking
Serviceberry	Oval	White	April	40	5-9	Has huge clouds of flowers, edible fruit
Silverbell	Round	White	May	30	5-8	Many clusters of bell-like flowers
Yellow-Wood	Rounded	White clusters	June	40	4-8	Very showy, fragrant flowers

Evergreens—These mainstays of every planned home landscape are beautiful throughout the entire year; are hardy, healthy growers; are available in different sizes, shapes and colors; are generally adaptable to most situations; and are very often misused by both beginning and old-time gardeners. The fault here lies in the fact that evergreen trees, as distinct from evergreen shrubs, can quickly grow into large trees where the gardener really wanted and expected a low, slow-growing shrub evergreen. There are, however, enough different evergreens with varied growing habits to allow the gardener to choose the one best suited to do the job and still be the one that will not outgrow its site.

For evergreens with horizontal branches and beautiful formal pyramidal or columnar shapes, select from the Douglas firs, spruces and the family of true firs. The pines and cedars are less formal in shape but also grow into magnificent specimen trees. Whatever your choice, remember that evergreens, while they are wonderful as backgrounds, hedges and foundation plantings, also provide year round green color that is a welcome break in the drab, almost colorless lanscape of winter and should be considered as specimen trees when planning and planting.

Mixture of evergreens and deciduous plants set off this difficult-to-landscape home

EVERGREEN TREES

Tree	Shape	Color	Height in Feet	Area	Remarks
Arborvitae					
American	Conical	Green	50	3-7	Good for landscape but discolors badly in winter
Cedar					
Atlas	Pyramid	Bluish	100	6-9	Very beautiful appearance
of Lebanon	Wide pyramid	Green	120	6-9	Famous in Bible
Cypress					
Arizona	Pyramid	Silver grey	40	6-9	Likes light, dry soil
Italian	Thin pyramid	Deep green	75	7-10	The cypress of history
Douglas Fir	Pyramid	Varies	300	5-7	Fine landscaping tree
Fir					
Nikko	Pyramid	Deep green	90	4-7	Best specimen fir
White	Pyramid	Bluish	125	3-8	Extremely hardy
Hemlock					
Canadian	Pyramid	Green	85	3-7	Also good for hedges
Carolina	Pyramid	Green	70	4-8	Excellent as specimen
Holly					
American	Round	Green	50	6-9	Some varieties better than others
English	Pyramid	Dark green	40	7-9	Need male and female for berries
Longstalk	Pyramid	Green	30	5-8	Looks like a pear tree

Evergreen Trees (Continued)

Tree	Shape	Color	Height in Feet	Area	Remarks
Juniper					
Chinese	Columnar	Green	60	3-9	Also available as shrub
Greek	Pyramid	Blue-green	60	7-9	Only grows in mild climates
Oak					
Live	Spreading	Green	60	7-10	Deciduous in northern part of area
Pine					
Austrian	Pyramid	Green	75	4-7	Good rugged looking tree
Eastern White	Pyramid	Blue green	100	3-7	Graceful as specimen tree
Mugho	Round	Green	8	2-7	Beautiful at entrances
Spruce					
Colorado Blue	Pyramid	Blue green	100	1-6	Dense, beautiful growth
Engelmann	Pyramid	Blue green	150	2-6	Smaller in cultivation
Norway	Pyramid	Dark green	100	2-7	Very dense grower
Yew					
English	Columnar	Dark green	60	5-7	Red, berry-like fruits in fall
Japanese	Various	Dark green	30	4-8	Fine tree, also shrub forms available

Fruit Trees—Don't be misled by the glowing reports in the nursery catalogs about how easy it is to grow your own fruit. Like so many other garden activities, you only get out what you put in. Fruit trees require more work and more attention than other trees, and, right at the outset, more care in selection.

Temperature and rainfall govern the kind of trees that will bear fruit, and the new gardener would be wise to stick closely to those varieties recommended for his area. Unlike other trees that may survive in a slightly colder or drier area than recommended, fruit trees will not bear fruit if the temperature and rainfall are not just right. For example, certain fruit trees will go through severe winters with no trouble, but will not set any fruit because the summers are too short for the fruits to mature.

Despite some of the stories you are bound to hear, few fruit-bearing trees are grown directly from seed. Instead of trying your luck with the peach-pit bit, spend a few dollars at a nursery and come away with a tree that will, in all probability, bear fruit for you to enjoy and brag about, right on schedule.

Speaking of bearing fruit on schedule brings us to the question of just when do young trees bear fruit. Fruit trees rarely bear fruit the first year after planting so keep that in mind before complaining to your local nursery man about "that tree you sold me."

Fruit	*Bears After (years)*	*Bears For (years)*
Apple	4-7	50+
Apricot	3-5	20+
Cherry (sour)	3-5	25+
Cherry (sweet)	4-6	50+
Citrus	3-5	25+
Currant	2-3	5+
Fig	2-3	25+
Peach	3-4	10+
Pear	3-5	50+
Plum	4-6	20+
Quince	4-6	20+

(Dwarf fruit trees bear earlier but do not live as long as standard trees.)

Fruit trees can also be barren for other reasons, including lack of or improper pollination. Without adequate or proper pollination many fruit trees will be full of blossoms, but when fruiting time comes, there will be no fruit. Those fruit trees that can pollinate their own blossoms and bear fruit are called self-fruitful and do not need other varieties of the same fruit for pollination. Self-unfruitful varieties should be planted with two or more varieties of the same fruit near each other if the tree is to bear fruit. Check the table which follows for recommended varieties and pollination information.

Fruit	Recommended Varieties	Pollination
Apples	Delicious Cortland McIntosh Jonathon Wealthy	Have satisfactory pollen, plant at least two different varieties near each other
	Baldwin Winesap Paragon	Unsatisfactory pollen, must be planted with varieties with good pollen listed above
Cherries 　Sweet	Bing Lambert Napoleon Black Tartarian	Self unfruitful, first three will not pollinate each other, so plant Black Tartarian for cross-pollination with each
Sour	Early Richmond Montmorency	Self-fruitful, may be planted alone
Peaches	Golden Jubilee Carman Elberta Afterglow	Self-fruitful, may be planted alone
Pears	Bartlett Clapps Favorite Bosc Anjou Seckel	Requires cross-pollination, plant with at least one other pear variety
Plums	Green Gage Burbank	Self-unfruitful, requires cross-pollination, plant with at least one other plum variety

New homeowners and beginning gardeners interested in having fruit-bearing trees on their property should investigate the dwarf fruit trees now offered by nurseries around the country. These trees, available in dwarf form of apple, peach, cherry and pear trees produce full-sized fruit on small-sized trees. These trees are ideal for the small property owner, allowing him to grow a variety of fruits without requiring the space, time and attention demanded by the larger full-sized trees. Instead of needing large spraying or dusting equipment and ladders for picking—dwarf trees allow the grower to reach every branch for both

Mature dwarf apple tree can be picked without a ladder

spraying and picking by merely stretching his arm. Though dwarf trees generally cost about twice as much as standard trees, they offer, in addition to the advantage of size for the small piece of property, a quicker bearing tree, since most bear one to two years earlier than standard-size trees.

One last item to remember when considering dwarf fruit trees for your property; these small trees can also be used as specimen trees in a landscape plan, espaliered into beautiful shapes and placed against walls, as fruit tree fences, or placed as accent plants along driveways or walks.

Pre-Planting Treatment—Many of the suggestions mentioned for the pre-planting treatment of shrubs (Chapter 5) also apply to trees, but there are some differences as well as some similarities worth discussing here.

Trees can be bought bare root, balled and burlapped, and container grown, with the transplanting method usually dictated by the size and variety of tree. Small trees up to ten feet tall can be transplanted successfully bare root, but almost all trees of a larger size should be transplanted with roots and earth ball intact. Certain trees, both large and small, should always be transplanted using the ball-and-burlap method. Included in this list are most evergreens and oaks, as well as beech, birch, sourwood, sweetgum, magnolia, dogwood, tulip-tree and several varieties of maple.

Though planting time is not as critical for trees with root balls as it is for bare-root trees, the best time to plant trees is early spring, with fall and early winter alternate times. Many local nurseries will plant trees bought from them at no additional charge, and this is the ideal situation. Don't be surprised if these experts suggest planting the tree at some time other than those recommended. With their skill, know-how and equipment, their chances of success are quite high at almost any time of the year. Trees that you buy and are going to plant yourself without professional help, whether with root ball or bare root, should be planted as soon as possible after they arrive at your home. If there will be a delay, certain precautions must be taken. Balled-and-burlapped trees should be placed in a cool, windless spot and the earth ball kept moist. Do not allow the earth or the roots to dry out or you will lose the tree before you plant it.

Bare-root plants that will not be planted immediately, should be unpacked, inspected and heeled into a trench and kept moist until they can be planted permanently. Choose a site for your heeling in trench that is out of the direct sun and wind, for both will dry out plants very quickly.

Though also discussed in Chapter 1, planning before planting is especially important when working with trees. It is far easier to remedy a planning error made with shrubs than it is with trees, for trees are bigger, more difficult to handle because of large root balls, and more susceptible to damage while being transplanted. When planting a tree, plan on doing it only once—pick a spot that will be the tree's permanent home.

To try and assure that planting is the first and last for each tree, lay out your property to scale on graph paper and position trees carefully on it before actually buying and planting. Consider that more trees will probably be desired and purchased in future years, so remember to plan for them. Be sure that trees will not crowd each other or buildings and that when planted and grown they will not block out desirable views.

PLANTING TREES

Techniques for planting trees are the same as for shrubs as discussed

Everything that's required to plant a balled-and-burlapped tree

Large hole is dug, then planting mixture is mixed in the bottom

When trunk is perfectly vertical, bindings are cut

Burlap spread in hole bottom will eventually rot

Supporting stakes are driven before hole is refilled

Give it plenty of water so soil settles all around roots

Protect young trees with tree wrap paper at least for first year

in Chapter 5. However, because of the difference in size, there are several additional things to think about when transplanting trees. These suggestions, when combined with the instructions for shrub planting, will practically guarantee success in transplanting trees.

1. Don't try to plant trees with trunks over four inches in diameter. This is a job for an experienced nurseryman. Trees of this size are too big to handle, require huge planting holes and too much manual labor for the beginning gardener.

2. Dig your planting hole about twice as wide and twice as deep as the earth ball. Fill the hole about half full of a well-mixed combination of topsoil and well-rotted manure and tamp well before placing the tree and earth ball into the hole.

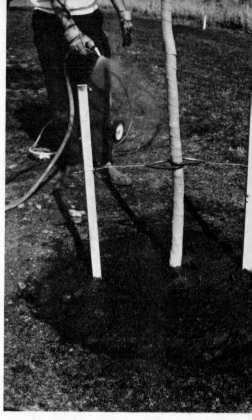

Fill saucer area with water and then water tree twice a week

Rubber or plastic loops over guy wire protects trunk from possible cuts

3. Young trees should be staked to maintain stability until the roots take hold in their new home. Drive the stake into the hole before placing the tree so that the roots are not cut or disturbed by the stake. Trees up to fifteen feet in height should be supported by two or three sturdy stakes and guyed with wires. Be sure the tender trunk is protected with rubber or plastic hose pieces so the wires do not cut into and damage the tree trunk.

4. When maneuvering the earth ball into the hole, or moving it at any time, pick it up by the earth ball and not by the tree trunk. Handle the tree and the earth ball carefully so they go into the ground intact and no roots are exposed or damaged.

5. Plant the tree at the same depth, give or take one inch, as it was

at the nursery. This can be done by checking the trunk for a soil mark. Be sure the tree is at the proper depth before starting to refill the hole. As you refill the hole, stand back several times, and at different positions around the tree make sure the tree is standing perfectly straight. If not, force soil under one side or the other until it is vertical. There are more enjoyable pastimes than filling in the hole, tamping down the earth and standing back to admire your handiwork—a crooked tree. Then, either the tree stays crooked or, more usually, you must dig out and replant the tree.

6. Fill the hole about half way and water well so soil can fill in around roots and eliminate air pockets that dry out the roots. Add more dirt and more water until the hole is filled to about two or three inches below ground level. Leave this saucer-shaped depression to hold rain water and keep the roots moist. Apply a layer of mulch to the saucer after it has been thoroughly watered, and keep this moist also.

7. Do not fertilize the first year, except with well-rotted manure mixed with the topsoil used to fill the hole. Fertilizing with chemical fertilizers, when trees are being transplanted, tends to burn the tender roots and can kill the tree or make it that much harder for the tree to become established.

Some trees can be planted as they come, basket and all

POST-PLANTING TREATMENT

There is not too much that the homeowner must do to keep his trees healthy and growing but, what there is is very important. Because you took this tree out of its "natural environment" and made it part of your landscape, it is up to you to see that the tree thrives—not just grows, but thrives. It is therefore, your responsibility to provide certain services so these trees become beautiful specimens.

Watering—Without proper watering newly-planted trees will not last long and established trees will slowly die. Proper water does not mean keeping the soil around the trunk of a tree soaked at all times (this too can kill a tree). It does mean providing enough water to the tree so it does not dry out.

Newly-planted trees should be watered for the first few weeks after planting, as well as through any drought periods during its first summer after transplanting.

All trees on the home property should get a thorough soaking once a week if rainfall has been insufficient. Soak for several hours with a soaker hose or bubbler attachment for best results.

Fertilizing—Feeding trees is a must if you are to keep them healthy and growing. The continual raking up of organic material, in the form of leaves, before they rot, robs the trees of their natural supply of food, and this must be replaced by chemical and organic fertilizers.

To repeat: newly-planted trees should not be fertilized until they have become well established, a period of approximately one year. After that time, a regular feeding with a complete fertilizer once a year will do the job very well.

Tree fertilizing is best done in the early spring, just as growth starts. But, it can also be done through early summer in most parts of the country. If this period has been missed, the trees may safely be fertilized in the fall, after all leaves have been dropped. Fall fertilizing is effective for all deciduous trees, but should be avoided for evergreens; they should be fed only in the spring.

Do not merely spread fertilizer on the ground around the tree trunk and think the job has been done. This does more harm than good. Surface feeding encourages shallow root growth which causes eventual weakening and damage to the tree. Holes between fifteen- and eighteen-inches deep and about the same distance apart should be drilled all around the tree, to a distance several feet past the end of the longest branch. Pour about ⅛ of a pound of complete fertilzier, say, 10-6-4 into each hole and water thoroughly. Do not over-fertilize. Over-fertilization will not make the tree grow faster, but may actually retard growth by burning the roots.

Staking—As stated before, all young trees six or more feet tall need support until they are firmly established and well rooted in the ground. Smaller trees can be supported by a single sturdy stake driven into the ground about a foot away from the trunk. Hold the tree to the stake with wire, after protecting the tree trunk by putting the wire through a piece of plastic or rubber hose. Do not allow wire to come in contact with the trunk or it will cut into and damage it.

Larger trees, those with diameters of up to about three inches, usually require two stakes, one on each side of the tree. Still larger trees, if they are not well established and are planted in such a location that they may be buffeted by strong winds, should be guy-wired to three stakes (like tent pegs) placed around the base of the tree at an angle, into the ground.

Pruning—This job, which seems to scare most new gardeners, is simple, if you follow the limits of good sense and several basic pruning rules. Cut out all diseased and dead branches and those live branches which cross over other live branches. Prune as close as possible to the tree trunk and do not leave stubs which will rot and offer entry into the tree for bugs and fungi. Remove only those branches that should be removed and don't feel you haven't done a good job if your pile of pruned branches is not high. Cover all wounds or pruning cuts with tree wound paint immediately after the cut is made, and renew the dressing as required to keep the area well protected.

For more detailed pruning and for pruning of large trees it is wise to call in a professional, for a few wrong cuts here and there on an otherwise healthy tree can injure the tree and often lead to its death.

INSECT AND DISEASE CONTROL

Insect and disease control are important to most trees and critical to some. While detailed information will be given in Chapter 10, several suggestions are made here for general preventive maintenance of most trees.

1. Dormant oil spray should be used for deciduous trees in early spring before the buds break, to kill any insects that have wintered over on the tree. Read directions carefully for this and all other insecticides and, for dormant spray, spray only when temperature will be above 40° for a 24 hour period.

2. Use all sprays, insecticides, miticides and fungicides, as directed on the container and do not mix your own "witches' brew" by combining several different chemicals. Though some mixtures may do no damage,

some chemicals are not compatible and the resultant spray may be disastrous to your plants.

3. Spray regularly and cover all parts of the plant—trunk, stems, leaves (both topside and underside) and fruit if there is any. Spraying once or twice a season will do little good. Spray every seven to ten days and after every heavy rainfall.

4. Fruit trees need to be sprayed a bit more carefully if pollination is to take place and the tree is to bear fruit. Spray fruit trees as soon as color appears on the buds and again just before the blossoms burst. Do not spray again until most of the petals have fallen, and then spray every ten days to assure best coverage and protection.

5. Check into the all-purpose sprays. They are especially valuable when you cannot identify the insect or fungus that is having a picnic with your trees. While this shot gun method is not the best, it does get results and, more often than not, your problem can be eliminated with regular sprayings of these chemicals.

Every garden plant worth planting is worth protecting, so keep up a steady, regular stream of sprays, throughout the summer and you will be assured of trees that are lovely to look at.

CHAPTER 7

Roses

The poetess Sappho elevated the rose to nobility when she wrote, in 600 B.C., in her "Ode to the Rose":

> "Would Jove a Queen of Flowers ordain,
> The Rose, the Queen of Flowers, should reign"

To prove it is the symbol of romance for lovers everywhere, rearrange the letters of rose, and you have Eros, the god of love. Roses were never associated with black magic, yet love potions always contained rose water or rose oil, flower of Venus, goddess of love. England was only one of the countries to use the rose symbolically in the War of the Roses; the red rose of the house of Lancaster vs. the white rose of the house of York. Included in numerous folk tales and legends are all manner of wonderous reports of sweet and innocent maidens being transformed into virgin white, or blushing pink roses.

Fascinating though these stories may be, they are far from the real reasons why you and I buy roses. It may be beauty, color, romance, or the desire to do the right thing that acounts for the initial attraction. Whatever your reason . . . you have plenty of company. The rose is by far the favorite garden flower in the United States and most other parts of the world.

But, stop a moment, and heed a word of caution. Remember, roses require and deserve special care and attention. While it is true that "anyone can grow roses," it is also true that there are *roses* and roses!

Most hardy rose bushes will survive if uncared for and ignored—but that's all they'll do. If you are willing to devote a short time each week, during the growing season, to your roses, you will be more than repaid. If you think that beautiful roses, like well-behaved children just happen, forget it—and save your money!

PLANNING FOR ROSES

Rose bushes are something special, so think ahead and plan their location. There are so many different varieties, types and colors that the new gardener can easily exhaust both his sanity and his pocketbook picking at random. The wisest and most economical solution is therefore, to plan before buying. What are the uses to which you want to put your roses? Are you planting them as specimen plants in a rose garden?; as an effective and beautiful entrance (draped onto and over an arbor or trellis)?; as a shrub or living fence that is not only beautiful but affords a measure of privacy and security from people, children and animals?; as a bed of flowers for a long season of almost continuous beauty and color?; to provide cut flowers for the house?; or as an unbeatable landscaping element? Plan first, because within its extensive family the rose can almost surely provide the type, variety, and color best suited to the job you have in mind. With the completed plan, you can select and buy the rose that will do you the most good while adding to the beauty and value of your property.

Whatever your decision, several points should be considered when selecting the location:

a) Sunshine. Roses do best with at least six hours of sunshine a day. They can do with less, but the resulting blossoms will be inferior.

b) Drainage. Roses require soil that is well drained, as noted in the chapter on Soil Conditioning.

c) Air Movement. Roses should be protected against unbroken severe windstorms, but conversely should not be so enclosed that there is limited air movement. Insufficient air movement will result in a never-ending battle with black spot and mildew.

d) Tree and shrub roots. Planting roses too close to trees and shrubs can cause a shortage of plant nutrients in the soil around the roses. Tree and shrub roots will absorb more and more nutrients, leaving less and less for the roses. A metal plate can be placed in the ground, to the depth of the offending roots to cut them off from the rose roots.

e) The remaining considerations for successful rose planting such as good soil, sufficient moisture, and feeding are controlled by the gardener and should not, unless conditions are extreme, be used as overriding factors in selecting rose location.

If you have enough space available, take a good, long look at it before laying out a rose garden. Look at the spot from many different angles, from the house (upstairs and down), and from the other vantage points on your property. Remember, it is not only the close-up look at the roses, but the overall appearance that makes for a truly lovely rose garden. While it is true that rose gardens may be of any size, it is best to set aside a reasonably large area for this purpose. Then the garden can have a definite shape and form to include walking paths of either well-kept grass or some sort of brick or stone, as well as the roses.

There are a great many things to think about when planning or laying out a rose garden. Some are common sense, while others are acquired through experience, but all require thought and careful planning. And, when planning, put it down on paper. On paper you can move, arrange, and rearrange the plants before actually lifting a spade.

As noted, the overall appearance and effect is important, so when doing your layout on paper, group together those roses that belong together. Make sure the flower colors look well side-by-side, that they harmonize, and that they are set off by a suitable background(not your neighbor's basketball backboard or washline). Consider the full-grown size of the rose bushes, so placement of individual bushes will add to the overall appearance. The whole idea is to blend all the elements in the rose garden into a pretty picture, and not to present individual plants in what looks like organized chaos.

If enough space is not available for this type of special, separate rose garden, you may still enjoy the beauty of single rose varieties; along a driveway, at an entranceway, or even in the case of tree roses, standing tall planted among the shrubs in an established flower bed. Wherever you plant your roses, be certain you are planting the best available in your area.

BUYING ROSES

Selecting healthy, disease-free plants is probably the most important step in successfully growing roses. There are no "bargain" roses but high price does not always mean superior roses. There are many roses of older varieties that are available at a lower price that are magnificent, strong growers, and often worth many times the selling price. Whatever the variety, buy it from a reliable, well-established nursery or mail-order nursery. Most growers and nurseries give a guarantee—if the plants do not grow or are otherwise unsatisfactory within 6 months, they will be replaced. For your own personal guarantee of success, select plants that are:

a) Grade 1 or 1½ (lower grades are inferior)
b) Rated high by the American Rose Society or named as All-American Rose Selections

c) Field grown (greenhouse plants are unaccustomed to outdoor conditions)

d) Properly packed and maintained moist.

Roses are either bare root or in containers, and some nurseries wax the dormant plants. Check bare-root roses to see that the root system is full, appears vigorous, and has not been allowed to dry out. Container roses allow later planting, and should be removed from the container carefully so the earth ball is undisturbed. Although waxed plants keep better than unwaxed ones in department stores or other warm salesrooms, they are not recommended for use in states such as Arizona because of the possibility of wax burn on the canes caused by hot weather following planting.

KINDS OF ROSES

The great variety of roses available can cause considerable confusion for first-time gardeners. The following guide tells the gardener what he wants to know and the best roses of each kind for his own garden. It is far from detailed or complete and is, of course, merely a beginning.

Hybrid Teas—This is the variety most people think of when roses are mentioned. Probably the best for the home garden, these roses are generally hardy in most climates, and feature long, usually pointed buds which become beautifully-shaped blooms. The height of the bush varies with the variety. A great many different colors are available, with more being added every year. The long lasting quality of the blooms makes them perfect for cutting as well as garden beauty. These are the roses usually sold by your local florist.

Hybrid Perpetuals—Larger and more massive than the Hybrid Tea, these roses were especially popular about 50 years ago. Extremely hardy, these roses are fine for areas with severe winters. The large, well-formed flowers are neither as delicate nor as perfect as the Hybrid Teas and are produced on heavy, long stems. Included among the best Hybrid Perpetual Roses are Frau Karl Druschki, Magna Carta, George Arends, and Ulrich Brunner.

Floribundas—Easily the most versatile of the rose varieties, the Floribundas are equally useful in rose gardens, as single specimen plants, as hedges and in flower beds. Growing in clusters, these roses require a bit less care than Hybrid Teas, and produce blooms in a wide choice of colors over a long full season. The Floribundas vary greatly in shrub size, some being almost dwarf, while others range upward to five- or six-feet tall. Whichever way they are to be used, Floribundas belong in everyone's home garden.

BEST HYBRID TEA ROSES

Name	A.R.S. Rating	Year of Origin	Color	Fragrance	Height in Inches
Crimson Glory	9.1	1935	Dark red	Heavy	30-48
Charlotte Armstrong	9.0	1940	Light red	Good	48 plus
Chrysler Imperial	8.8	1952	Dark red	Heavy	30-48
Tropicana	8.5	1963	Orange red	Heavy	30-48
Tallyho	8.2	1948	Light red	Heavy	30-48
Rubaiyat	8.2	1946	Light red	Heavy	30-48
Etoile de Hollande	8.1	1919	Medium red	Heavy	30-48
Dainty Bess	8.4	1935	Light pink	Heavy	30-48
Pink Favorite	8.2	1956	Medium pink	Light	30-48
First Love	8.0	1951	Light pink	Light	48 plus
Royal Highness	7.9	1963	Light pink	Light	30-48
Golden Wings	8.5	1956	Medium yellow	Good	30-48
Eclipse	8.1	1935	Medium yellow	Light	30-48
Kings Ransom	7.7	1962	Deep yellow	Heavy	48 plus
Lowell Thomas	7.7	1944	Deep yellow	Heavy	30-48
Burnaby	8.1	1935	White	Good	30-48
White Wings	7.5	1947	White	Little	30-48
Pedralbes	7.4	1935	White	Heavy	30-48
Peace	9.6	1945	Yellow blend	Little	30-48
Tip Toes	8.9	1948	Pink blend	Heavy	30-48
Tiffany	8.8	1954	Pink blend	Heavy	30-48
Helen Traubel	8.7	1951	Pink blend	Heavy	48 plus
Mme H. Guillot	8.4	1935	Red blend	Heavy	48 plus
Saturnia	8.1	1936	Red blend	Light	30-48
Sutter's Gold	8.1	1950	Yellow blend	Good	48 plus
Sterling Silver	7.0	1957	Mauve	Heavy	30-48

10 points—perfect rose
9-10—outstanding variety
8-8.9—Excellent
7-7.9—Good
6-6.9—Fair

117

Grandifloras—The most recently introduced class of roses, the Grandifloras, combine the attributes of the Hybrid Teas and the Floribundas to produce clusters of perfectly formed Hybrid Tea-type blooms. The large tapered blooms appear on tall vigorous stems, in almost unbelievable profusion. The Grandifloras are considered by many to be the best and easiest roses to grow.

Polyanthas—Very hardy, these roses produce a goodly number of blooms, but they are quite small. Because of their size, these roses are fine for perennial flower beds or for color in shrubbery borders. One of the best Polyantha roses is the short, white Pinafore.

Climbers—These roses grow on extremely long canes, so they are a natural for use on arbors, trellises, fences and pergolas. Trainable into smooth flowing shapes, climbers grow better with horizontal training than vertical. When ordering climbers, be sure to clearly indicate that you want climbers, since many varieties of Hybrid Teas and Floribundas come in both climbing and bush types.

Tree Rose—These are really bush roses grafted onto a stiff trunk or standard. The roses produced are large and almost exact replicas of the bush types, but come from an umbrella-like mass of beautifully lush, healthy foliage at about waist or shoulder height. The trees are sturdy (but should be staked) and are especially dramatic, eye-catching speci-

Tree roses can be protected by staking to ground and covering with mulch during winter

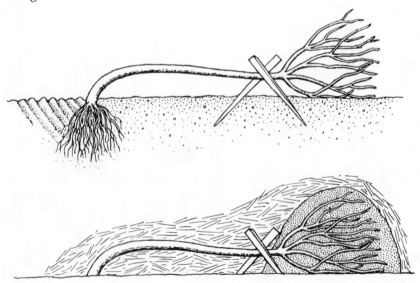

BEST FLORIBUNDAS

Name	A.R.S. Rating	Year of Origin	Color	Fragrance	Height in Inches
Carrousel	9.0	1950	Deep red	Good	24-36
Eutin	8.6	1940	Deep red	Light	24-36
Frensham	8.6	1946	Deep red	Light	30-48
Red Pinocchio	8.6	1947	Deep red	Heavy	24-36
Spartan	8.5	1954	Orange red	Heavy	30-48
Betty Prior	9.0	1935	Medium pink	Good	24-36
America's Jr. Miss	8.6	1964	Light pink	Good	24-36
Else Poulsen	8.3	1924	Medium pink	Light	30-48
Pink Bountiful	8.2	1945	Medium pink	Heavy	24-36
Starlet	7.4	1957	Medium yellow	Light	24-36
Goldilocks	7.3	1945	Medium yellow	Good	under 24
Ivory Fashion	8.0	1958	White	Heavy	24-36
Moonsprite	7.7	1956	White	Good	24-36
Fashion	9.0	1947	Pink blend	Light	24-36
Border Gem	8.6	1961	Pink blend	Good	under 24
Little Darling	8.4	1956	Yellow blend	Light	over 36
Vogue	8.2	1949	Pink blend	Heavy	over 36

BEST GRANDIFLORAS

Name	A.R.S. Rating	Year of Origin	Color	Fragrance	Height in Inches
Montezuma	8.6	1955	Light red	Light	30-48
Starfire	8.0	1958	Medium red	Good	30-48
Roundelay	8.0	1954	Dark red	Good	30-48
Queen Elizabeth	9.0	1954	Medium pink	Good	48 plus
Golden Girl	7.4	1959	Medium yellow	Good	30-48
Buccaneer	7.3	1952	Medium yellow	Good	48 plus
June Bride	7.5	1957	White	Good	48 plus
Pink Parfait	7.6	1960	Pink blend	Heavy	30-48
Floriade	7.3	1963	Orange blend	Good	30-48

BEST CLIMBERS

Name	A.R.S. Rating	Year of Origin	Color	Fragrance
Paul's Scarlet	9.1	1915	Medium red	Light
Chevy Chase	8.9	1939	Deep red	Good
Etoile de Hollande	8.6	1931	Deep red	Heavy
Crimson Glory	8.3	1945	Deep red	Heavy
New Dawn	8.8	1930	Light pink	Light
Cecile Brunner	8.5	1894	Light pink	Heavy
Blossomtime	8.3	1951	Medium pink	Good
City of York	8.6	1945	White	Heavy
White Dawn	8.5	1949	White	Good
Sun Gold	8.6	1939	Medium yellow	Good
Paul's Lemon Pillar	8.2	1915	Light yellow	Heavy

BEST MINIATURES

Name	A.R.S. Rating	Year of Origin	Color	Fragrance
Red Imp	8.9	1951	Dark red	Light
Dwarf King	8.3	1957	Medium red	Good
Robin	8.1	1956	Medium red	Light
Sweet Fairy	8.3	1946	Light pink	Good
Baby Betsy McCall	8.2	1960	Light pink	Good
Tinker Bell	8.1	1954	Medium pink	Light
Pixie Gold	7.6	1961	Medium yellow	Light
Little Scotch	7.6	1958	Light yellow	Good
Cinderella	9.0	1952	White	Light
Twinkles	8.2	1954	White	Good
Peachy	8.2	1964	Pink blend	Good
Baby Masquerade	8.1	1956	Red blend	Light
Silver Tips	8.1	1962	Pink blend	Light

men plants. Where winters are severe, tree roses must either be potted and brought indoors, or covered and protected. Special attention should be paid to the area of the graft when protecting for the winter. Included among the best tree roses are Queen Elizabeth, Tropicana, Peace, Mister Lincoln, Camelot, Charlotte Armstrong, and Mirandy.

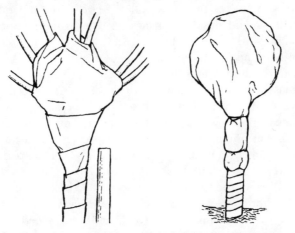

Graft or knob of tree rose must be protected throughout winter

Miniatures—Among the other roses that merit a short description are miniatures. The others are living-fence roses, and old-fashioned roses.

Miniature roses are perfectly named—they grow only eight- to twelve-inches high. Everything about these charming roses is proportionately scaled down, so the tiny leaves and blooms always look nice in pots, on borders, or even in rock gardens.

Living-Fence Roses—These everbloomers spread to form a hedge or fence. The roses produced by these bushes are small but prodigious in comparison to other roses, and the overall effect of a hedge or living fence covered with small roses can be breathtaking.

"Old-Fashioned" Roses—These were favorites for many years before the appearance of Hybrid Tea Roses. Not quite as perfect or pretty as the Hybrid Teas, many are worth having in your garden for their fragrance alone. Interesting roses in this classification are the Moss Roses, Provence, Bourbon and Damask Roses.

PLANTING ROSES

More poor defenseless roses are ruined or killed at planting time than at any other time, although the tragedy often does not become known until much later. Planting roses is neither difficult nor complicated, but requires more than just digging a hole and sticking the plant in the ground.

Roses can be planted in either the spring or fall (if bare root plants are fully dormant) or if potted plants are used, once good growth has started. The exact planting time will vary with location and temperature extremes. A rule of thumb to follow is: if local temperatures do not go below 10°—plant anytime bushes are dormant; if temperatures do not go below – 10°—plant early in the spring or in fall before the ground freezes; and if – 10° temperatures are frequent in your locality—plant only in the spring, and then just as soon as the ground is workable.

Under most normal conditions, roses do not need special soil preparation. However, loose, well-drained soil with organic material such as humus or peat moss gives the best results. If you are planning a large rose garden, you might want to change the present soil for new topsoil mixed with humus or peat moss. Single roses can be planted without prior soil preparation, but it is a good idea to exchange the soil from the hole with new topsoil and organic matter at the time of planting.

If your mail-order roses arrive at a time when you cannot plant them immediately (such as during the week and your schedule only allows gardening on week-ends), open the package and sprinkle the plants, especially the roots, with water. Then reclose the package and store in a cool, dark place (temperatures between 32° and 50°). This will keep the plants in good condition for about one week and then they should be planted.

If, however, for some reason you cannot plant them within a week, dig a trench in the garden large enough to accommodate all the bushes. Unpack the roses, lay them (roots, canes and all) into the trench and cover with at least six inches of soil. Mosten the soil thoroughly. If you do this quickly and correctly, the plants will remain in good condition for several months.

Of course, it is best to plant roses immediately upon their arrival. Open the package and check for broken or damaged roots or canes. Cut away damaged parts and prune roots that are considerably longer than the others. Place the roots in a pail of water containing a small amount of soluble fertilizer (check the package label for correct amount). Let the bushes stand in the pail of water for about one hour. Carry them, still in the pail, to the planting site. This soaking is beneficial to the roses for at least two reasons; it lets them really soak up water and nutrients before going into the ground, and it protects them from usually fatal drying effects of the wind, sun and air.

O.K., now dig—and I mean dig! Make the hole nice and roomy, big enough for the roots to be spread out and not cramped and bunched together. The hole should be at least 18-inches deep and approximately the same width. If you are planting several rose bushes at one time, mark off your spade at the correct depth and use it as you would a ruler or yardstick. Remember, don't be skimpy with the hole—generosity will pay off in a better rosebush.

Before you actually remove the first shovelful of dirt, place some heavy canvas, paper, or a basket next to the digging site. Use one of

Spread roots over inverted dirt cone

Check graft height; it should be exactly at ground level

these for the soil you dig since this soil will be replaced with a soil/humus combination. You can then get rid of the old soil without marring the lawn with clumps and clods of earth. The new mixture is made up of at least one part peat or leaf mold to three parts of soil. If manure is used, the proportion becomes one part well rotted manure to six parts of soil. Do not use fresh manure—it will injure the roots. Instead, use either well-rotted cow manure or the dehydrated, deodorized cow manure generally available.

Cloth keeps soil from messing up lawn area

Tamp firmly leaving depression around each bush

Water thoroughly and then refill saucer or depression

Mound this mixture at the bottom of the hole to form an inverted cone. Place the rose bush roots over the cone and spread them out and all around. Check the height of the graft (the knuckle or knob) and make sure it is at ground level. If it is above or below, redig and recone until it is right. In very cold regions, the knuckle should be about two inches below ground level.

With the rose bush atop the cone and the roots spread out, start to refill the hole while firming the soil around the roots with your fingers. This is a good "togetherness" project. While your wife or helper carefully starts to recover the roots, pressing and firming to eliminate any air pockets, you can catch your breath from having dug that hole. When the hole is about one third filled up, gently but firmly tamp down the

Right and wrong depths for planting roses

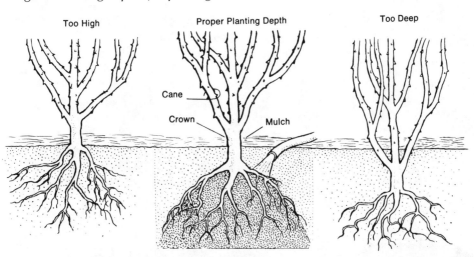

soil with your foot. Then fill the hole with the solution in which the roses were soaking. Allow the water to soak in (again, to eliminate any pockets) then fill with the remainder of the water mixture. When the soil reaches ground level, again tamp gently but firmly all around. Form a shallow indentation around the bush to catch additional water and rain.

Mound soil around the canes to a height of at least six inches, to protect the canes until new growth starts. When new growth starts, this mound can be leveled. After the rose bush has been planted, water well, and continue to water for several days.

To plant potted roses, follow the same steps outlined for bare-root roses, except there is no need for the soil mound at the bottom of the hole. Soak the pot soil so it will hold together when you remove the ball from the pot. If possible, without damaging the earth ball, check that the roots at the bottom have not become entangled or matted. If they are, fix and spread them out when placing the ball in the hole. Then continue with the same procedure used for bare-root roses.

For best results, the following spacing for the various kinds of roses is suggested:

Hybrid Teas	
Grandifloras	Approximately 2 feet apart
Floribundas	
Climbers	Approximately 8 feet apart
Creepers	
Shrubs	Approximately 3 feet apart

These distances are suggested for normal climates and growing seasons. Where the climate is milder and the growing season longer, proportionately greater spacing should be allowed.

WATERING

Roses thrive in moderate weather if they have an adequate supply of water. The key is "adequate" water. Roses do not do well with too much or too little water. A good system, during the growing season, is to water at least once a week, and water well. The water should penetrate the soil to a depth of at least one foot. Don't make the mistake of watering for a little while several times a week and think this is as good as one good watering—it is not. Such watering will probably do more harm than good. The best device for watering roses is a soaker hose, which squirts and soaks directly into the ground. Overhead watering is not recommended because it will not only wash off your spray protection, but the water remaining on the foliage is an open invitation to black spot and other rose diseases.

FERTILIZING

Roses are hearty eaters, so feed them well and often. In the case of new, large rose gardens, if the soil was prepared several weeks prior to putting the bushes into the ground, the recommended addition of about eight pounds of superphosphate or bonemeal per one hundred square feet should carry through until late summer. Chemical fertilizers should not be added to the soil at planting time. If manure is added at planting time, be certain it is well rotted. However, even well-rotted manure should not come in contact with the plant's roots.

Roses, other than new roses, should be fertilized early in the spring, and then two more times during the season. The second feeding is made around the end of June, or after the first bloom, and the third late in August. Do not fertilize later than the end of August, since this will induce new growth, and the new growth will be killed by the first frost. Use about a half cup of complete growth fertilizer per bush at each feeding, either formula 5-10-5, 7-8-5 or 10-10-10. Just about the easiest way to fertilize the individual rose bushes is to measure out the fertilizer into your hand, and then sprinkle it in an even circle around the plant, about six to eight inches from the plant. Cultivate the fertilizer into the ground to a depth of no greater than two or three inches, and water generously. Do not fertilize roses immediately after a rain, or at other time when the foliage is wet. If chemical fertilizer should happen to fall on the wet leaves, the foliage will probably become burned.

Bonemeal or dehydrated cow manure are marvelous, mild fertilizers for roses. However, since these organic fertilizers take some time getting to the plants, apply them very early in the spring or late in the fall. In the case of bonemeal, an application in the fall will affect rose growth the following spring, and not before. About three good handfuls of bonemeal should be sprinkled around each plant, cultivated in, and then watered well.

Winter protection: soil mounded about bush covered with available mulch

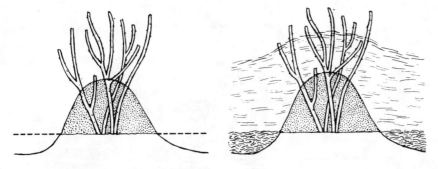

MULCHING

As we said previously, mulching serves a great many purposes, all beneficial to the plants. Not only do mulches make the garden or planting area look neater and better groomed, but they also maintain soil temperatures in summer and winter and they help keep weeds down and go a long way to maintaining moisture in the soil.

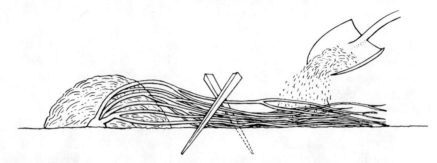

Climbers with unsteady support should be staked to ground and covered with soil for winter

Since mulching is one of the easier, if not the most rewarding gardening jobs in terms of unpleasant work saved, it should be done im-

Fenced climber mounded with soil then protected with discarded Christmas tree over winter

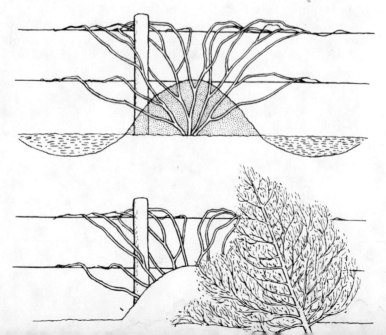

mediately after the roses have been planted. Lay the mulch down all around the rose plants and even it out so it becomes a level carpet about three-inches thick. If peatmoss or sawdust is used, they must be wet thoroughly before applying to the soil surface. All mulching materials should be watered heavily after aplication, and subsequent waterings should be into the mulch and not onto the foliage.

CUTTING AND PRUNING

Cutting roses for display and arrangement requires very little skill and even less experience. However, a few suggestions may help the beginning gardener get bigger more beautiful blooms from healthier bushes. First, never use anything but a very sharp knife or pruning shears when cutting roses. Never twist or snap a flower from the plant. It may be marvelous to watch in a Hollywood movie, but this kind of treatment will probably ruin the flower and certainly hurt the plant.

Though the recommendation was different in the past, it is now generally considered best to cut roses in the late afternoon. Flowers from first year plants should be cut with as short a stem as possible, so the plant may continue to manufacture food and grow, by utilizing as many leaves as can be left intact. Obviously therefore, blooms produced by older, better established bushes can be allowed a longer

a. Cut all faded blossoms from rose bushes
b. Proper method and length to cut most roses

Aphids actually sucking the life from a rose bud

stem. Cut bloom bearing stems only as long as you need them, and make the cut just above a node with a leaf made up of five leaflets. This will assure you of enough foliage still left on the plant to produce vigorous healthy growth. Always be sure to "clean house" in your rose garden as often as necessary. Remove all faded flowers and old blooms before they set seed. This prevents them from sapping valuable strength from the plant.

Roses are pruned to grow bigger better blooms on a healthier, stronger, more attractive bush. The danger in pruning is that if done incorrectly it can result in a badly damaged or dead plant. Each kind of rose bush has its own growth habits, so make sure you know what you are doing before you go at them with a pruning tool.

Pruning should be done in early spring, just as the buds begin to swell. Use sharp, clean pruning shears and cover the cut ends on the larger canes with tree wound paint.

Hybrid Teas are pruned back to about twelve to eighteen inches. Remove all dead wood, canes that cross, and those which do not conform to a pleasing or healthy bush shape. Make the pruning cuts just above an outside bud, so new growth will go outside and keep the center of the bush open and airy.

Floribundas and Grandifloras require a minimum of pruning, so merely remove dead wood, prune out crossing canes and shape as desired.

Climbers should be pruned only to remove those canes that will most probably cause tangling as time goes on. Remove old flower clusters and the oldest canes as well as dead wood, and generally keep them pruned to within bounds.

Tree roses should be cut back rather severely—all healthy canes should be cut back to less than ten inches from the trunk, at varying heights to give the tree a pleasant umbrella-like appearance when in bloom.

CONTROLLING INSECTS AND DISEASES

Roses get their share of diseases or disfiguring insects. To combat insects and diseases, set up a regular, once weekly spraying program, and stick to it. Use a multipurpose rose spray for a "one shot—takes care of everything" preventive program. To do justice to the most prevalent disease and insects, the spray should contain an insecticide (such as sevin or malathion) a miticide (such as kelthane) and a fungicide (such as maneb or ferbam).

Prune out all dead wood and cut back roses only in spring

Spray your rose bushes late in the afternoon when it is cool, but early enough to allow the spray to dry. Use a lightweight, simple sprayer, with an extension nozzle so you can be sure to get both sides of the leaves, from the ground up. Whatever chemical or type of sprayer you use, do a thorough job and do it regularly. After a heavy rainstorm, start from scratch and spray thoroughly all over again.

This program of minimum labor will, under most conditions, assure you of healthy, disease-free roses. If you cannot give the bushes this little bit of care, and devote this minimal amount of time to them once a week, don't grow roses.

CHAPTER 8

Flowers

To many people, flowers are what gardening is all about. Who can or wants to argue with them? What is there to rival the sweet beauty or delicate fragrance of flowers fresh from the garden? Where else can you be assured of finding exactly what suits your taste and fancy, no matter the direction your fancy may wander?

From the almost endless list of flower varieties available at most nurseries and garden centers, the new gardener, if he has done his homework well, can choose plants, seeds, and bulbs for flowers that bloom in succession around the year—this without the aid of roses, considered in a class all their own. Then, according to what he wants and considers most important, he can have beautiful and colorful flowers outdoors around his house and property, fresh flower arrangements indoors, or both.

Because of the almost unbelievable variety of flowers available the new gardener must do a bit of learning if he hopes to get the most from the flowers he plants. It is not enough to like the color, aroma or shape of flowers before planting them recklessly throughout your landscape. Of equal importance are the height, kind of plant, growth habit, period of bloom and other considerations.

KINDS OF FLOWERS

To the uninitiated, flowers are flowers. Most are grown from seed or bulbs, bloom and then die. Some come back year after year, while some seem to refuse to bloom at all, even the first year. A more careful look at the world of flowers reveals that they are divided into groups, by the way they live and die and from what they grow. Generally speaking (it must be general because some plants shift from one group to another

Flowers on both sides of fence make a beautiful scene

in certain climates and under certain conditions) flowers are broken into distinct groups—annuals, biennials, perennials and a group made up of bulbs, tubers, corms and rhizomes.

To all practical intents and purposes, annuals take a single year to complete a full life cycle—they are planted in the spring, bloom in the summer and die in the fall. Except for those that reseed themselves, annuals will not grow again the second season unless deliberately replanted.

Biennials take twice as long to complete the full life cycle because they require a cold weather induced dormant period between leafy growth and blooming. So again, barring the ever present exceptions found in nature, biennials are planted in the summer, kept alive though dormant through the winter, then flower the following summer, set seed and die in the fall. Though it does not take two calendar years, it does take two summers, hence the name biennials.

Perennials continue the spread of time required to complete a life cycle. Grown one season, they wither in the winter and spring to life again the following year, so perennials can be counted upon to live for at least two years. Many perennials live on indefinitely, while others flourish for several years and then deteriorate and die.

To be categorized correctly, bulbs, tubers, corms and rhizomes belong with the perennial flowers, for they come back and flower year after year. Common usage has put them in a class of their own, and despite the protests of true botanists, that's where they will stay. Actually, bulbs are food storage centers for underground stems from which will grow the next season's plants. In bulbs the food supply surrounding the stem takes the form of fleshy scales, for corms it is solid rather than scaly. Corms and bulbs have growing points at the top from which the bud, stem, and eventually the flower grow, as well as base plates that produce the roots. Tubers have no base plates, are solid, thick underground stems with eyes or buds on the top and sides from which the stem and roots develop. Rhizomes are also thick underground stems, but with these, the bud or eye is on the top (at the end or at a joint) and the roots grow from the bottom. Though this description may sound quite botanical and perhaps complicated, the difference is important when planting and is easily determined when you hold one or another in your hand.

FLOWER-GARDEN PLANNING

Without reiterating the suggestions and comments found in Chapter 1, it should suffice to say that the more planning and learning the new homeowner does before planting, the better will be his attempts at landscaping, especially when it concerns flowers. Indiscriminate planting of flowers and indeed of anything else results in a hodge-podge effect, if that is an effect at all.

Started in winter when it's too cold to do much more than think about gardening, the selection of flowers for your garden can be a fascinating and educational pastime, employing your own preferences and prejudices, neighbor's recommendations, compromise, book knowledge, and, in later years, your own experience. By carefully working out a selection of those flowers best suited to your purposes, and experimenting with them, you will have the most fun and the best-looking flower garden.

Some of the items to keep in mind when selecting flowers are: height (from a few inches to several feet), color (just about every color in the rainbow), time of bloom (different flowers come into bloom at various times over a nine-month period), growing requirements (from light to heavy watering, from shade to full sun, from poor soil to rich soil), growing habits, hardiness and, of course, where and how they are going to be used.

Grouped jonquils add color to garden dead spot

A few general rules may help you in getting set for your flower elimination contest:

1. Flowers are most effective when grouped—several of a single variety in a relatively small area. A single plant, standing alone, will rarely be effective enough to warrant anything more than a passing glance.
2. Find out the mature height of the plants and place low growing ones in front and tall varieties in the rear.
3. Flowers will stand out better and be more attractive when placed in front of a green background. Especially in borders or other semiformal or formal gardens use evergreen shrubs or other dense green plants as background material.
4. If flowers are primarily for cutting, plant them away from the house where the cut stems will not detract from the appearance of the house or other plantings.
5. Keep the overall effect in mind at all times. Clashing colors, overpowering varieties and plants with unsightly growing habits can ruin an otherwise beautiful garden. It is better to use less rather than more color and, in almost all cases, restraint and taste result in the best effect.

6. Remember the other parts of the plant as well as the flowers when planning. Foliage and stems can neither enhance or detract from an otherwise nice planting.

7. Balance your enthusiasm with the knowledge of what plants look like before, during and after flowering. If they do not fit in with the overall plan, relegate them to cutting gardens or other out-of-the-way spots.

8. Balance, too, all the elements of the planting. Colors, sizes and types should be balanced for pleasing effect, but not to the point of fanatical symmetry.

9. Don't expect to be able to buy or grow every flower that appeals to you. Too much of anything is usually no good, so select the best and show them off to their best advantage.

10. Select flowers with a good chance of growing in your locality, especially in borders or foundation planting. Experiment with different varieties and select from these the additions or substitutions for the old standbys you've developed.

*Textures and tones makes this a
real garden spot*

NINE MONTHS OF FLOWERING BEAUTY

	Name	Color	Type
FEBRUARY	Crocus Aureus Chrysanthus	Orange White, yellow	Bulb
	Eranthis Cilicica Hyemalis Tubergenii	Yellow	Bulb
	Galanthus Elwesii Nivalis Florepleno Plicatus	White	Bulb
MARCH	Anemone (Windflowers) (Atrocaerulea)	Many Blue	Bulb
	Chionodoxa Luciliae Sardensis	Blue Blue	Bulb
	Crocus Biflorus Sieberi Tomasinianus	Many Lavender Lavender	Bulb
	Hyacinths	Red, pink, white	Bulb
	Leucojum Vernum	White	Bulb
	Muscari Botryoides	Blue	Bulb
	Tulip	Many	Bulb
APRIL	Alyssum	Yellow	Perennial
	Anemone (Apennina)	Blue	Bulb
	Candytuft	White	Perennial
	English Daisy	White, pink	Biennial
	Fritillaria	Many	Bulb
	Iceland Poppy	Many	Biennial
	Leucojum Aestivum	White	Bulb
	Muscari Plumosum Tubergenianum	Violet Blue	Bulb

Nine Months of Flowering Beauty *(Continued)*

Name	Color	Type	
Narcissus Daffodils Jonquils Narcissi	White, yellow	Bulb	**APRIL** *(Continued)*
Primrose	Many	Perennial	
Puschkinia	Light blue, white	Bulb	
Scilla	Many	Bulb	
Virginia Bluebells	Blue	Perennial	
Bleeding-Heart	Pink rose	Perennial	**MAY**
Camassia Esculenta Leichtlinii	Blue Blue	Bulb	
Candytuft	White, lilac	Annual	
Canterbury Bell	Many	Biennial	
Columbine	Many	Perennial	
Forget-Me-Not	Blue, white	Perennial	
Iris (Dutch)	Many	Bulb	
Jupiter's-Beard	White, crimson	Perennial	
Lilium (Lilies)	No blue	Bulb	
Meadowrue	White, lilac	Perennial	
Muscari Comosum	Mauve	Bulb	
Pansy	Yellow, purple	Annual	
Peony	White, pink	Perennial	
Phlox	White, pink	Perennial	
Red-Hot Poker	Yellow, red	Perennial	
Wallflower	Red, yellow	Biennial	

Nine Months of Flowering Beauty *(Continued)*

	Name	Color	Type
JUNE	Allium Chives Karataviense Moly	Lavender Pink Yellow	Bulb
	Baby's-Breath	Pink, white	Annual
	Balloon Flower	Blue, white	Perennial
	Bellflower	Blue, white	Perennial
	Canna	Red, yellow	Bulb
	Daylily	Many	Perennial
	Dianthus	Many	Annual
	Everlasting	White	Perennial
	Flax	Gold, blue	Perennial
	Forget-Me-Not	Pink, blue	Annual
	Foxglove	Red, white	Biennial
	Hollyhocks	Many	Biennial
	Iris (Spanish)	Many	Bulb
	Lupine	Blue	Annual
	Monkshood	Blue	Perennial
	Pansy	Many	Biennial
	Pentstemon	Red, purple	Perennial
	Poppy	Red, pink	Annual
	Portulaca	Many	Annual
	Rudbeckia	Yellow	Annual
	Scabiosa	Blue	Annual
	Spider Lily	Yellow	Bulb
	Spurge	Yellow	Perennial

Nine Months of Flowering Beauty *(Continued)*

Name	Color	Type	
Statice	Pink, blue	Perennial	**JUNE**
Stock	White, blue	Annual	*(Continued)*
Stokes Aster	Mauve	Perennial	
Sundrops	Yellow	Perennial	
Sweet Alyssum	White, violet	Annual	
Sweet William	Red, pink	Biennial	
Thistle	Blue, white	Perennial	
Washington Lupine	Many	Perennial	
Ageratum	Blue	Annual	**JULY**
Astilbe	Pink, white	Perennial	
Begonia Tuberous	Many	Bulb	
Calendula	Gold	Annual	
Clarkia	Rose, purple	Annual	
Clematis	White, blue	Perennial	
Coreopsis	Yellow	Annual	
Dahlia	Many	Annual	
Delphinium	Many	Perennial	
Four-O'Clock	Pink, white	Annual	
Galtonia	White	Bulb	
Impatiens	White, pink	Annual	
Iris (English)	Many	Bulb	
Larkspur	Many	Annual	
Marigold	Gold, red	Annual	
Morning Glory	Purple, blue	Annual	

Nine Months of Flowering Beauty *(Continued)*

	Name	Color	Type
JULY *(Continued)*	Nasturtium	Yellow, red	Annual
	Petunia	Many	Annual
	Plantain Lily	Mauve, white	Perennial
	Polianthes	White	Bulb
	Salvia	Blue, red	Annual
	Sneezewort	Yellow	Perennial
	Speedwell	Blue, white	Perennial
	Spider Plant	Pink	Annual
	Sunflower	Gold	Annual
	Zinnia	Many	Annual
AUGUST	Allium Odrorum	White	Bulb
	Acidanthera	White	Bulb
	Amaranthus	Red	Annual
	Aster	Many	Annual
	Chrysanthemum	Many	Perennial
	Gaillardia	Red	Annual
	Globe Amaranth	White, purple	Annual
	Phlox	White, pink	Annual
	Scilla Tubergiana	Light blue	Bulb
	Snapdragon	Many	Annual
	Strawflower	White, red	Annual
	Tigridia	Red, yellow	Bulb
SEPTEMBER	Anemone	Pink, white	Perennial
	Bachelor's Button	Blue	Annual

Nine Months of Flowering Beauty *(Continued)*

Name	Color	Type	
Cockscomb	Yellow, red	Annual	**SEPTEMBER**
Cosmos	Many	Annual	*(Continued)*
Crocus Zonatus Medius	Red lilac Lilac	Bulb	
Tritonia	Red, yellow	Bulb	
Colchicum Autumnale Speciosum	Purple Lilac	Bulb	**OCTOBER**
Crocus Speciosus	Blue	Bulb	

This chart lists only the better known and easiest to grow bulbs. Since many varieties bloom over periods of more than a single month, the month of greatest profusion is noted here. Similarly, only major colors are listed, except where a full range exists, hence the word "many."

ANNUALS

Of all the flowers, and perhaps even of all the plants, annuals are the easiest to grow, produce the greatest mass of color and are the least expensive. Unfortunately, these attributes cause them to be mistreated or, more accurately, not treated at all. Because they are easy to grow, many gardeners tend to plant them and forget them, not realizing they require care and attention if superior flowers are to be achieved. The large mass of color often hides poor garden housekeeping and because annuals are inexpensive they are not fed, watered or weeded as are more expensive and longer lasting flowers and plants. Annuals are too useful and too beautiful to be treated in such an offhand manner; with a little care and attention they become truly grand additions to every home landscape.

Requirements—Because annuals have minimum requirements, many gardeners think they can grow anywhere, without further care. It's true, many can, but the result is usually tall, skinny plants with a few scraggly flowers. Treat the soil for annuals as you would for any other plant, tree or shrub, making sure it is loamy and not too heavy, well fertilized, adequately drained and thoroughly mixed with organic matter. If annuals are included in the overall landscape plan the flower beds will also contain bulbs, perennials and shrubs, so do the soil conditioning job once before planting, and do it thoroughly so it nourishes all the plants and gives you the best results. A word of caution concerning fertilizer for annuals and other flowering plants: do not overdo, especially when using fertilizers high in nitrogen. A high nitrogen fertilizer will cause considerable foliage growth—unfortunately at the expense of flowers. A complete fertilizer, such as 5-10-5, well mixed into the soil will produce the best balance of leaves and flowers.

ANNUALS FOR POOR SOIL

Cockscomb (Celosia)	Nasturtium
Coreopsis (Calliopsis)	Petunia
Four-O'Clock	Poppy (California, Corn)
Gaillardia	Portulaca
Love-Lies-Bleeding (Amaranthus)	Sweet Alyssum

Most annuals prefer sunny locations if they are to produce the greatest number of blooms, though some grow and prosper in partial shade.

ANNUALS THAT GROW IN SHADE

Cockscomb (Celosia)	Impatiens (Balsam)
Coreopsis (Calliopsis)	Stock

ANNUALS THAT GROW IN PARTIAL SHADE

Candytuft	Lupine	Snapdragon
Clarkia	Pansy	Sweet Alyssum
Forget-Me-Not	Phlox	Verbena
Larkspur	Poppy (California)	

Regular watering too is important to most annuals. Because it is impossible to depend on summer rainfall, except to occur at exactly the time you least want it, be prepared to water annual flower beds at least once a week or when they appear to need it. Water thoroughly when you water, but do not water until the soil becomes waterlogged. Soaker hoses are best for watering flower beds since the water goes directly into the soil and not onto the leaves where it may encourage certain diseases. Check the soil in the beds often and when the soil becomes dry, but before it starts to crack, lay in a soaker hose and water thoroughly. As to the care of the beds themselves cultivation while good for many plants, can hurt annuals. Cultivate the soil around the plants only until the plants are a few inches tall. Cultivation after this point will injure roots and damage the plants. Mulching between and around the plants keeps weeds down and conserves the moisture in the soil.

This is a good place for clean, weed-free grass clippings—they make a fine mulch for annuals.

ANNUALS FOR VERY DRY AREAS

Coreopsis (Calliopsis)	Morning Glory	Salvia (Sage)
Four-O'Clock	Phlox	Sunflower
Larkspur (Delphinium)	Portulaca	Zinnia

Planting—Just about all annuals are started from seed sown outdoors, with a very few showing better results if planted indoors and then transplanted outdoors as seedlings. Timing is extremely important whichever way you start the seeds. Neither seeds nor seedlings should be planted, with a few exceptions listed here, until all danger of frost is past. Seeds will not germinate until the temperature reaches about 60° and sowing them too early, in the often damp spring, causes many to rot. Some seedlings are extremely susceptible to frost and planting them too soon can cause severe damage instead of the good head start for which you hoped. Some annuals can be planted successfully at other times of the year beside spring, coming into their own after one or two seasons, as indicated in the list below.

FALL-SOWN ANNUALS

Calliopsis (Coreopsis)	Morning Glory
Candytuft	Poppy (California)
Clarkia	Sage (Salvia)
Four-O'Clock	Sunflower
Larkspur (Delphinium)	Zinnia

Detailed instructions for planting annual seeds are found on each packet of seeds. These directions should be followed exactly along with several other suggestions offered here.

For broadcast planting, prepare the soil, scatter the seed evenly (that's broadcasting) in the area in which you want it to grow, barely cover the seed with soil by gently raking, water and wait for flowers. Do not drench the area with water—it may wash away the seed. Do not cover the seed with a heavy layer of soil, most annual seeds are very tiny and are unable to push their way through. If the soil is very heavy or cakes easily, add a soil conditioner, like vermiculite, to the soil to give the seeds a fighting chance for survival. Once the seeds start to sprout, thin them to the desired distance recommended for that particular plant.

Making your own seedlings for transplanting can be a lot of fun, but it

Transplanting petunias in bloom in peat pots

can also be a lot of work. For those interested in making their own seedings, the process is the same as described in Chapter 9. For those who do not wish the bother of making seedlings but do want the advantages they offer, local nurseries can supply healthy seedlings for most transplantable annuals. Remember though, seedlings are tender babies, and must be given tender, loving care until planted outdoors.

ANNUALS BEST SOWN AS SEED WHERE THEY ARE TO GROW

Larkspur (Delphinium)   Portulaca
Lupine   Stock
Nasturtium   Sunflower
Poppy (California)   Sweetpea

One more group of annuals requires mention here—the annuals that set and sow their own seed so they reappear in the same area for many years. Nothing is done to these annuals to help them achieve this feat—just sit back and wait and they will return.

SELF-SOWING ANNUALS

Ageratum*

Baby's-Breath (Gypsophila)

Bachelor's Button

Calendula (Pot Marigold)

Clarkia

Cockscomb (Celosia)

Cosmos*

Dianthus (Chinese Pink)

Four-O'Clock

Gaillardia*

Larkspur* (Delphinium)

Love-Lies-Bleeding (Amaranthus)

Lupine

Marigold*

Pansy

Petunia*

Poppy

Portulaca

Snapdragon

Strawflower

Sweet Alyssum

Zinnia*

* (Will bloom following spring-summer)

Pinching Back—Several annuals are improved considerably if they are pinched back (cutting or pinching off the tip of the shoot or the terminal bud with the fingers or fingernail) at an early stage in their development. These annuals unless pinched back grow to· be tall and

Dahlias show beauty and symmetry of nature

Small edged area used to display pretty flowers

spindly, producing few flowers. Pinching off the shoot tip after the plant has a few sets of leaves on its main stem causes the plant to produce additional healthy side shoots and become quite healthy and thick.

ANNUALS TO BE PINCHED BACK

Ageratum	Dianthus	Snapdragon
Calendula (Pot Marigold)	Petunia	Verbena
Chrysanthemum	Phlox	Zinnia

Cutting—Intelligent, careful cutting of annuals will give you beautiful flowers for indoor arrangements without harming the plant. Indeed, many annuals increase their flower output after several have been picked.

GOOD ANNUALS FOR CUT FLOWERS

Ageratum*	Cosmos	Nasturtium*	Snapdragon
Amaranthus	Gaillardia	Pansy	Stock*
Calendula	Gypsophila	Phlox*	Strawflower
Calliopsis	Larkspur	Pinks*	Sunflower
Clarkia	Lupine	Poppy	Sweetpea*
Chrysanthemum	Marigold	Scabiosa*	Verbena*
			Zinnia

* (Has nice fragrance)

POPULAR ANNUALS FOR THE HOME GARDEN

Name	Color	Height	Spacing in Inches	Sow/Blooms	Requirements	Use	Remarks
Ageratum	Blue and others	10-14"**	9-12	3/7#	Full sun-partial shade	Edging	Reseeds self each year
Amaranthus (Love-Lies-Bleeding)	Deep red and others	4"**	18	5/8##	Full sun, poor soil	Bedding	Good in hot dry areas
Aster	Many	20"	10	3/8#	Full sun, well-drained soil	Bedding	Blooms for 6 weeks
Baby's-Breath (Gypsophila)	Pink, white	12"	6	4/6##	Full sun	Trim for arrangements, edging, borders	Can be dried
Bachelor's Button	Blue and others	24"	12	6/9##	Full sun-partial shade	Cut flowers	Many varieties
Calendula (Pot Marigold)	Gold and others	24"	12	4/7##	Good soil	Bedding	Blooms over long time
Candytuft	White, lilac and others	16"	12	3/5##	Full sun, well-drained soil	Edging, borders	Good foliage
Clarkia	Rose, purple	24"	10	5/7##	Partial shade	Cut flowers	

149

Popular Annuals for the Home Garden (*Continued*)

Name	Color	Height	Spacing in Inches	Sow/ Blooms	Requirements	Use	Remarks
Cockscomb (Celosia)	Yellow-red	24"**	18	3/9##	Full sun-partial shade, well-drained soil	Borders	Can be dried
Coreopsis (Calliopsis)	Yellow and others	1-3'	12-15	4/7##		Cut flowers, bedding	Long blooming
Cosmos	Many	3-6'	18-24	4/9#	Sandy soil	Background	Cut flowers
Dahlia	Many	18-24"	18	3/7#	Full sun, well-drained, loamy soil	Bedding, cut flowers	Tubers also available
Dianthus (Chinese Pink)	Many	12"**	6	4/6##	Fertile, well-drained soil	Edging, borders	Hardly, easy to grow
Firebush	—	30"	18	5/9##	Full sun	Border hedge	Turns red in fall
Forget-Me-Not	Pink, blue and others	20"	9	4/6##	Partial shade, water	Border, cut flowers	Not good in heat
Four-O'Clock	Pink, white and others	24"	12	5/7##		Bedding	Grows well in poor soil
Gaillardia	Deep red	2"**	10	4/8##	Full sun, well-drained soil	Cut flowers, dry flowers	Very showy

Popular Annuals for the Home Garden (*Continued*)

Name	Color	Height	Spacing in Inches	Sow/ Blooms	Requirements	Use	Remarks
Globe Amaranth (Gomphrena)	White, purple and others	18"	12	5/8##	Full sun	Dry for ever-lasting flower	
Impatiens	White, pink and others	18**	12	5/7##	Full sun-partial shade, water	Bedding	Easy to grow
Larkspur (Delphinium)	Many	2-4'	10	3/7##	Cool weather	Screens	Cut and dry flowers
Lupine	Blue and others	3"	12	3/6#	Full sun, good soil	Borders	Cut flowers
Marigold	Gold, red and others	10-40"	12	5/7##	Full sun-partial shade, good soil	Cut flowers	Easy to grow
Morning-Glory	Purple, blue and others	Vine		5/7##	Sandy soil	Screen	Soak seed before planting
Nasturtium	Yellow, red	Climber	12	4/7##	Full sun, poor soil	Bedding	Strong odor
Pansy	Yellow, purple	8"	8	1/5#	Partial shade, water	Bedding, cut flowers	
Petunia	Many	10"	6	4/7##	Full sun-partial shade	Bedding	Loads of flowers

Popular Annuals for the Home Garden (*Continued*)

Name	Color	Height	Spacing in Inches	Sow/ Blooms	Requirements	Use	Remarks
Phlox	White, pink and others	18"	6	5/8##	Full sun-partial shade	Bedding, cut flowers	Good hot weather plants
Poppy	Red, pink and others	3'	12	11-3/6##	Full sun	Borders	Cut flowers
Portulaca	Many	10"	6	4/6##	Full sun, dry soil	Rock gardens, ground cover	Self sow
Rudbeckia	Yellow	2-3'	18	4/6##	Full sun	Cut flowers	Likes heat, black-eyed susan
Salvia (Sage)	Blue, red and others	24"	12	3/7#	Full sun	Cut flowers, masses	Pretty blues
Scabiosa	Blue and others	3'	12	4/6##	Full sun	Cutting	Easy to grow
Snapdragon	Many	2'**	12	3/8#	Full sun, water	Bedding	Long blooming, popular
Spider Plant	Pink and others	3-4'	15	4/7##	Full sun, sandy soil	Borders, bedding	Long blooming
Stock	White, blue and others	1-3'	10	4/6##	Full sun-partial shade, good soil	Cut flowers	Good bedding, plant

152

Popular Annuals for the Home Garden (*Continued*)

Name	Color	Height	Spacing in Inches	Sow/ Blooms	Requirements	Use	Remarks
Sunflower	Gold	7-12"**	2 feet	4/7##	Full sun	Screens	Easy to grow, birds love seeds
Strawflower	White, red and others	30"	12	5/8##	Full sun	Dried flowers	
Sweet Alyssum	White, violet	10"	4	4/6##	Full sun-partial shade, well-drained soil	Useful many ways	
Sweet Pea	Many	Climber	8`	3/6##	Well-drained, good soil, water		Beautiful color, aroma
Verbena	White, red	10-20"	10	3/8#	Full sun, good soil	Cut flowers	Good as edging
Zinnia	Many	10-36"	9-12	5/7##	Full sun	Cut flowers	Bedding

**Other Sizes Available.
##Sow Seed Outdoor/Month of Bloom.
#Month of Start Indoors/Month of Bloom.
(Example—4/8 = April/Blooms August.)

BIENNIALS

Largely ignored by most gardeners, new and old alike, the biennial group contains some of our prettiest flowers. Though they are not permanent and for this reason perhaps less appealing, it is unwise to ignore such beauties as Canterbury bell, hollyhock, foxglove and forget-me-not.

Only a few brief notes are necessary to describe the planting and care of biennials, but this, again, does not mean they should be neglected. Easily transplanted, biennials can be purchased as seedlings from a local nursery or planted as seeds either indoors in pots or in a coldframe and transplanted outdoors on cool, cloudy days.

Since it takes biennials two years to reach flowering maturity, gardeners should expect no flowers the first year. The initial year is given over to producing foliage, and the second year to flowering, setting seed and dying.

All biennials prefer open sunlight and rich soil that has been liberally laced with organic matter. They must be watered carefully because, though they thrive in moist soil, puddles do little to improve them. Other requirements parallel those of annuals and perennials and these should be heeded carefully for best results.

PERENNIALS

"Something for everyone" could be the advertising slogan for perennials if, indeed, perennials needed advertising. Nowhere else in nature is there such wide variety in every important characteristic as there is in the herbaceous perennials (as opposed to "woody" used to designate trees and shrubs which are also perennials). Any gardener to inclined can, by poring over catalogs and reference books, find, within reason, exactly the type of plant he has in mind.

Included in this large grouping, omitting for now, bulbous perennials that are treated independently, are plants that are tall, medium and short; colors that try the imagination including some not in the rainbow; flowers in every size, shape and form; fragrances from delightful to deadly; and growth habits that encompass all conditions imaginable. But for all of this, perennials are a bargain, because they come back year after year, they save time, money and work for the gardener. Although a bit more expensive initially than most annuals or other plants, perennials are ultimately cheaper because they last longer and often multiply.

It is easy to see why perennials are such favorites with gardeners and

POPULAR BIENNIALS FOR THE HOME GARDEN

Name	Color	Height	Spacing	Blooms	Requirements	Remarks
Canterbury Bell	Many	1-4'	12"	March-April (South) May-June (North)	Partial shade, well-drained, rich soil	Beautiful and showy
English Daisy	White, pink, red	6"	8"	Spring	Full sun, well-drained, good soil	Good with bulbs
Forget-Me-Nots	Blue, pink, white	9"	6-8"	Spring	Partial shade	Dense carpet for borders
Foxgloves	Red, purple, white	3-6'	12"	June	Partial shade, good soil	May reseed self
Hollyhock	Many	6'	24'	June	Full sun-partial shade, well-drained soil	Reseeds self very well
Iceland Poppy	White, red, yellow, orange	2'	12"	April	Well-drained soil	Fine for cutting
Pansy	Blue, purple, red, yellow	9"	8"	June, July	Well-drained soil, cool	Long bloom time
Wallflower	Red, yellow	2'	12"	May, June	Well-drained soil	Pinch back
Sweet William	Red, pink	1-2'	10"	June	Little heat	Easily propagated

why no landscape can be considered complete without them. A word of caution. Like any other plants, perennials cannot be used indiscriminately. Putting them on your overall plan, in places where they grow and show off best can save you considerable amounts of time and money. Remember also that since almost all perennials disappear in the winter and start growing again early in the spring, they should not be used as replacements for evergreens or in places requiring year round backgrounds, foliage or separation.

Flowers in masses make the prettiest show

Requirements—Though most perennials are not especially fussy about where they are to grow, the fact that they come back year after year warrants some soil improvement before they are planted. The reason for this is simple. It is difficult, if not impossible, to greatly alter the conditions of the soil once perennials are permanently installed. Since most perennials do best in soil that is well drained, reasonably fertile and neither hard packed nor sandy, be prepared to do whatever is necessary to bring the soil up to meet these minimum requirements, before planting time.

Turn over and prepare the soil, in which the perennials are to be planted, to a depth of about two feet. Adding organic matter (peat moss or well-rotted manure) does the trick nicely. Do not add large quantities of powerful, low organic fertilizers to the soil immediately before planting, they can do severe damage by burning the plant's tender roots. Check the soil, by a soil test, for the level of acidity present and supply additives as required to either raise or lower the pH level. Most perennials do well in a neutral or nearly neutral soil, and major variations in the pH level will retard growth and flowering.

Every year after planting, perennials need fertilizer feedings to keep them healthy and blooming. Early in the spring, just as the plants start their annual comeback, and again in early summer, work some complete fertilizer, say 5-10-5 into the soil and water well. Do not work the fertilizer too deeply into the soil for roots can be damaged by the cultivating tool and you will have defeated your own purpose. Further feedings in the latter part of the summer are not recommended as they promote new young growth which is extremely susceptible to winter-kill.

Since the majority of perennials thrive under "normal" conditions, only the exceptions are noted here. All other plants can be assumed to do well under conditions mentioned as general requirements.

PERENNIALS FOR POOR SOIL

Alyssum (Goldentuft)	Dianthus (Some varieties)	Speedwell
Candytuft (Evergreen)	Phlox (Moss)	Spurge
Daylily	Sage (Salvia)	Thistle

A small number of perennials do well in shade or light shade, while others require full sun all day long. As a general rule, perennials do very well and bloom as expected with approximately half a day of sunlight. Therefore, select the perennials for your garden according to the site you have available and the amount of sunlight the area gets during the course of a normal day.

PERENNIALS FOR SHADY AREAS

Balloon Flower	Meadowrue	Primrose
Bleeding-Heart	Monkshood	Speedwell
Candytuft	Phlox	Virginia Bluebell
Christmas Rose	Plantain Lily	

As is the case with most other requirements, perennials do best with enough but not too much water, with exceptions that do well in dry areas and others that do well in abnormally moist areas. For the majority, a thorough watering at least once a week is sufficient to keep the plants growing and blooming. Light sprinklings do no good for perennials or any other plants. If rainfall is lacking, water the perennial garden once a week, preferably in late afternoon (to limit evaporation) and water well.

PERENNIALS FOR DRY AREAS

Coreopsis	Statice
Dianthus (Grass Pink)	Spurge
Poppy (Iceland)	Thistle

Mulching the perennial garden or border is always a good idea because of the triple threat-ability of most good mulching materials. Peat moss, buckwheat hulls or grass clippings make good mulches. Water the entire area before putting down the mulch, spread the mulch about three-inches deep, and then water thoroughly once again. Use only those mulching materials that do not become matted; thickly matted mulch can exclude rain water.

In many areas of the country, great temperature variations cause alternate freezing and thawing of the soil and this, in turn, can cause heaving of perennial roots and exposure to the elements. To prevent this, and keep the ground frozen throughout the winter, apply a three- to four-inch layer of mulch directly over the plant and, if possible, over the entire garden area. If the withered plant stalks are cut back to three or four inches before mulching, they will help keep the mulch in place despite winter winds. Do not mulch until the ground is frozen. Wait until it is thoroughly frozen and apply mulch that is clean and weed free.

Cultivating the soil shortly after planting also helps keep the weeds down and maintains the moisture level. Remember not to cultivate too deeply or the roots will be damaged. Light cultivation every once in a while, if there is no mulch present, should keep the soil from crusting and make the soil more attractive and more receptive to the retention of water.

Planting—The different ways of propagating perennials are almost as numerous as the number of perennials themselves. The new gardener should be content to grow his perennials from seed, from locally supplied seedlings or, after a few years, from cuttings or by dividing old clumps. The best rule to follow, at least until you are experienced and can make your own rules, is to start perennials from seed only when the kind and variety you want are unavailable at a local nursery. Usually, the plants available at reputable nurseries are healthy, ready to be planted and inexpensive. If you prefer to start your perennials from seed either indoors or out, the procedures described for vegetables (Chapter 9) plus the instructions on the seed packet will start you off on the right foot.

Perennials should be planted either in the spring, once the soil has warmed up, or in the early fall, when enough time still remains for the plants to become established. After planting, pay strict attention to regular watering. Plant roots are small and unable to absorb sufficient quantities of water immediately after they have been planted. In this instance they should be watered more often, rather than in one large soaking. Once established, water well, but do not drown.

After your perennials have been growing, in the same spot, for several years, replanting, transplanting and dividing should be considered. If you have treated your plants well, they will respond with lush growth and beautiful flowers. For awhile they will grow increasingly more dense, but then will become overcrowded and finally start a gradual decline in looks and flowering. Many perennials can be rejuvenated and multiplied by division, that is, the actual cutting of the clumped roots into sections and replanting as separate plants. Division and transplanting is best accomplished in the spring for plants that bloom in

Solid bands of plants can accent large lawn areas

late summer and fall, and in the fall for plants that bloom in the spring. A few plants like lupine, baby's-breath and peony do not take kindly to being moved and are best left alone.

When moving, dig out the plant carefully so as not to damage any more roots than necessary, and cut into sections. Retain only the healthiest portions of the clump and discard all others. To keep the clumps from drying out while reconditioning the soil, lay them in a trench or hole in the soil and cover with moist soil or peat moss. Replant the divided clumps as quickly as possible and continue to water well until they are established.

Staking—Many perennials grow very tall and become top-heavy at blooming time. If left to their own devices, they will bend or topple over in the first strong wind. To avoid this, plants that are known to grow tall should be provided with stakes for support. These stakes are usually made of bamboo, wood or metal sometimes painted green and are available at your local nursery or some hardware stores. To protect the plant's roots, once the plant has become established, place the stakes while the plant is young. When the plants reach a good height, but before they start to bend, loosely tie the stalks to the stakes, using a soft-tying material. Never use uncovered wire or other materials that can cut the tender stalk. Tie the material, green raffia or plastic covered thin wire are best for the job, securely to the stake and then loop it loosely around the stalk. Leave enough room around the stalk for the plant to expand as it grows.

Remember there is nothing especially pretty about the stakes, so use them sparingly—just enough to do the job. For some plants, like peonies, ready-made rigid wire supports are available, and these are placed around the plant for support.

Cutting—Two purposes are served by cutting perennials as they flower and immediately after they flower. Cutting, and this of course means judicious cutting, gives you beautiful flowers for indoor arrangements and also spurs the plant to produce additional flowers and leaves. All faded flowers should be removed from plants as soon as possible so the production of seed heads is limited. Since the natural life cycle includes reproduction, the plant will expend its energy making seed once the flower has bloomed. Cut off the faded flower or group of flowers as soon as the bloom starts to fade, but do not cut off leaves. The plant, through its leaves, will continue to manufacture food and additional flowers, thus extending the blooming season. Removing faded blooms will also keep the plant from looking unsightly.

POPULAR PERENNIALS FOR THE HOME GARDEN

Name	Color	Height	Spacing in Inches	Blooms	Requirements	Use	Remarks
Alyssum	Yellow	12-15"	12	April-May	Full sun	Borders	Flowers and leaves useful
Anemone	Pink, white	1-3'	9-12	September-October	Partial shade, good, well-drained soil	Cut flowers	Not hardy in severe winters
Astilbe (Spirea)	Pink, white and others	Various	10-15	July	Partial shade, water	Borders	Feathery flowers
Balloon Flower	Blue, white	15-24"	10-14	June-August	Full sun, well-drained soil	Borders, rock garden	Very pretty
Bellflower	Blue, white	8"-2'	12	June-July	Full sun	Cut flowers	Easy to grow
Bleeding-Heart (Dicentra)	Pink, rose	10"-1'	12	May-July	Partial shade	Edging, cutting	Long time favorite
Candytuft	White	10-15"	Spreads	April	Full sun, well-drained soil	Edging, rock garden	Can be cut also
Christmas Rose	White	12"	12	Winter	Shade, organic matter	Can bloom Xmas under snow	Poisonous
Chrysanthemum	Many, no blue	1-4'	12	July	Full sun, well-drained soil	Cut flowers, background	Many, many varieties
Clematis	White, blue	3-4'	18	Summer	Full sun, good well-drained soil	Borders	Fragrant

Popular Perennials for the Home Garden (*Continued*)

Name	Color	Height	Spacing in Inches	Blooms	Requirements	Use	Remarks
Columbine	Many	12-30"	12	May	Full sun-partial shade	Rock garden, cut flowers	
Coreopsis	Yellow	1-2'	15	July	Full sun-partial shade, well-drained soil	Cut flowers	Good mass border
Daylily	Many	1½-4'	2 feet	June	Full sun-partial shade, well-drained	Borders, cutting	Withstands most extremes
Delphinium	Many	To 60"	15	Summer	Good fertile soil	Borders, cutting	Needs care
Dianthus	Many	4-18"	Some spread	June	Full sun, sandy well-drained soil	Edging, cutting	Includes pinks, Sweet William
Everlasting	White	1-3'	12 feet	June	Full sun-partial shade, dry soil	Ground cover, cutting	Good foliage
Flax	Gold, blue, white	1-2'	12	June	Full sun, light soil		Continuous bloom
Forget-Me-Not	Blue, white	12"	6	May	Full sun-partial shade	Rock garden, ground cover	Very popular
Iris	Many	1-3'	12-18	May	Full sun, well-drained soil	Borders, cutting	Innumerable varieties
Jupiter's-Beard	White, crimson	3'	2 feet	May	Full sun, poor soil	Borders	Old-fashioned favorite

Popular Perennials for the Home Garden (*Continued*)

Name	Color	Height	Spacing in Inches	Blooms	Requirements	Use	Remarks
Meadowrue	White, lilac and others	1-4'	12-24	May-June	Partial shade, water	Borders, cutting	Nice foliage
Monkshood	Deep blue, white	3-5'	9-12	June	Full sun-partial shade	Cut flowers	Roots poisonous
Pentstemon	Red-purple	1-4'	12	June	Full sun	Cut flowers	After flowering cut back
Peony	White, pink and others	18"-4'	18	May	Full sun, good soil		Beautiful flowers
Phlox	White, pink and others	10"-3'	12-24	May-June	Partial shade, light soil	Rock gardens, edging	Some especially fine varieties
Plantain Lily	Mauve, white and others	1-3"	1-2	July	Full sun-shade, water	Cutting, showy foliage	Very long lived
Poppy	Many	1-3"	15	June	Full sun, good soil		Very showy flower
Primrose	Many	4-12"	6-14	April-June	Partial shade-shade, water	Various	Pretty plants
Red-Hot Poker	Yellow, red	2-4'	12-20 feet	May-October	Full sun, light soil	Display, cutting	Very showy flowers
Sage (Salvia)	Blue, white	2-4'	12-24	June-August	Full sun-partial shade		Several hundred varieties

163

Popular Perennials for the Home Garden (*Continued*)

Name	Color	Height	Spacing in Inches	Blooms	Requirements	Use	Remarks
Scabiosa	Blue, white	18-30"	10-12	June-September	Full sun, light soil	Borders, cutting	For warm climates
Sneezewort	Yellow	1-2'	10-14	June-September	Full sun, well-drained soil	Cutting	Heavy aroma
Speedwell	Blue, white and others	1-5'	10-15	July	Full sun-partial shade	Borders	Very showy
Spurge	Yellow	20-40"	10-15	June	Full sun-partial shade	Borders	Good foliage
Statice	Pink, blue	1-3'	10-15	June	Full sun, sandy soil	Cut and dry	Excellent for the seashore
Stokes' Aster	Mauve	10-20"	1 foot	June-September	Full sun	Cut flowers	
Sundrops	Yellow	8-18"	10-12	June	Full sun		Good bloomer, large flowers
Thistle	Blue, white	3-5'	12-18	June-August	Full sun, good soil	Cutting	For large gardens
Virginia Bluebells	Blue	12-18"	12	April-May	Shade, water		Very pretty plant
Washington Lupine	Many	2-4'	15	June	Partial shade, water		Very showy

BULBS

The first and last to bloom, bulbs rank high as all-time favorites in the hearts of gardeners and everyone who loves beauty. By opening and closing the growing season, bulbs tell us first that spring is on the way, and nine months later that winter is here. Nowhere else in nature can so much beauty and so many flowers be found. Known to man from the earliest days of recorded history, bulbs have been in and out of favor: sometimes worthless, other times worth thousands of dollars per bulb; sometimes praised other times cursed; sometimes admired and sometimes eaten. Today we find it hard to imagine a garden or home without at least a few bulbs.

As noted earlier in this chapter, the category of plants commonly called bulbs is correctly made up of bulbs, corms, tubers and rhizomes. For the purposes of the home gardener, it is sufficient to know that all of these are simply food storage centers for underground stems from which the next season's plants will grow.

SELECTING BULBS

Here again, if you wish nothing more than the common and the usual, the task of selecting bulbs for your garden is simplified by the listings in newspapers, garden magazines and nursery catalogs. It is truly a pity

You don't have to be Dutch to love tulips

Huge cannas are exquisite when grouped

though, to forgo the excitement and pleasures of seeing a truly magnificent flower growing in your garden simply because you did not know as much as you could have about what you were buying. While nothing will replace a reputable dealer, either local or mail order, it certainly is to your advantage to have a reserve of information at your fingertips.

Bulbs are generally graded for selling according to size and it is best to buy only graded bulbs. Though sometimes useful for mass planting, ungraded bulbs are usually worth exactly the low price paid for them. Akin to the way eggs are graded, bulbs for such flowers as tulips, crocus, hyacinths and narcissus (daffodils and jonquils) are graded from large to small—top, large, medium and small. Others, such as lilies, begonias (tuberous) and anemones have the following additional groupings: fancy, giant or extra large. Gladiolus uses jumbo to designate the largest bulbs and numbers from 1–6 to indicate the other grades; 1 being the largest after jumbo and 6 being the smallest grade. A good general rule to follow is to buy the largest bulbs you can afford. Although this may mean buying fewer bulbs those you plant will produce the very best flowers on the sturdiest stems. Hyacinths are an exception; with these bulbs, the word *exhibition* denotes those used for forcing indoors (more about that later) and *bedding* indicates those usually used in the garden. To avoid disappointment: buy carefully and know what you are buying; stay away from wild bargains; and put your trust and repeat business in the hands of reputable dealers.

FRAGRANT BULB FLOWERS

Acidanthera	Hyacinth	Narcissus
Amaryllis	Hymenocallis	Polianthes
Daffodil	Lilium	Tulip

REQUIREMENTS

Growing bulbs is neither overly simple nor fanatically exacting. It is exacting, however, in one area—water. While almost all bulbs will grow well in most types of soil, ranging from medium-heavy clay to very-sandy loam, they will do nothing worthwhile if drainage conditions are not correct.

Simply stated, if the soil in which you plan to plant your bulbs does not drain adequately and quickly, find another place to plant them. Bulbs will rot in soggy soils. This does not mean however that bulbs do not need moisture for best growth—they do. As a matter of fact they need a great deal of water, especially in the spring as they start to grow and in the fall as they store food for the following year.

As particular as they are about drainage, bulbs are not at all particular about the kind and quality of the soil in which they grow, provided sufficient plant nutrients are available. Before planting bulbs into a permanent bed, turn over the soil and include in the turning process a healthy layer of organic materials as indicated in the chapter on soil conditioning. If at all possible, prepare bulb beds several years before actual planting and include a good organic fertilizer, inorganic fertilizer, natural organic materials and limestone. If this is impossible and the bulbs are to be planted the same year as the soil conditioning, use only well-rotted organic materials in the soil and be very sure they are well mixed with the soil. Check the pH of the soil; since bulbs prefer soil that is on the alkaline side, add limestone as is necessary to all soil with pH lower than 6.5.

Fertile soil produces the best and biggest flowers, so add fertilizer to the bulb beds every year. Early autumn fertilizing is recommended for most bulbs as this is the time they store food for the next year's growth. Never allow the fertilizer to come in contact with the bulb or bulb roots.

Spring-flowering bulbs (winter hardy and planted in the fall) like full sun, but also do very well in partial shade. There is little problem of placing these bulbs so they get the most sunshine possible, for when they bloom in early spring, most trees are still budding and there are few leaves to block off the sun. Summer flowering bulbs (the frost-tender bulbs planted after all danger of frost) need full sun if they are to reach the maximum in full flowering beauty.

BULBS FOR SHADY AREAS

Allium	Eranthis	Lilium
Amaryllis	Fritillaria	Muscari
Anemone	Galanthus	Scilla
Begonia	Hippeastrum	Zantedeschia
Camassia	Leucojum	

Bulbs thrive in mulched beds because the possibility of heaving is greatly reduced and they need not fight weeds for available nutrients. Timing is very important here, for placing the mulch at the wrong time promotes growth that is killed by a late frost in spring. (Early mulch placement keeps the soil warm, causing the bulbs to start a growth cycle). Beds are mulched in the fall only after the ground is frozen hard, and not until then. Do not remove the mulch in the spring until the bulbs start to break through, and then replace with clean mulch once the shoots are well on their way.

Planting—Bulb planting is not the exact science some would have you believe, but it is not a hit or miss proposition either. When planting just a few bulbs a trowel will do an adequate job but, there is a better way. Using a special bulb planter gives you a hole with a flat bottom as opposed to the tapered bottom hole you get by using a trowel. When large bulbs are planted in a trowel hole, an air pocket is invariably left under the bulb and this can cause the bulb and/or its roots to dry out and die. With the flat bottomed hole produced by the bulb setter, the bulb rests directly on the soil in the hole bottom, eliminating the possibility of damaging, or killing, air pockets.

When planting small quantities of individual bulbs, it is best to place them in holes dug into previously conditioned soil, otherwise the hole you dig will probably cut right through your meager layer of topsoil and the bulb will rest atop some low-grade subsoil. If it has been impossible to precondition your soil, some measure of help can be given the individual bulbs as they are planted. Dig the hole at least six-inches deeper than recommended for the type of bulb being planted. Fill the bottom six inches with good topsoil, place the bulb atop it and cover with more rich topsoil. Most bulbs will flower well the first year planted regardless of the standard or quality of the sub or lower soil. However without the nutrients furnished by rich soil, all succeeding years' blooms will become poorer and poorer until blooming stops completely.

For mass planting of bulbs, another system is usually used. With this plan you dig out the entire bed to the prescribed depth, level off the soil, mark the rows or position of the bulbs, place them and then cover with topsoil. Here too, if the soil has not been preconditioned, dig it out deeper, fill to planting level with rich topsoil, place the bulbs and recover with topsoil.

Naturalizing is another technique used extensively with bulbs and consists of planting the bulbs in grass patches, on slopes, in rocky areas, just as they would grow in nature. For this kind of planting, do not lay out any lines or patterns, toss a handfull of bulbs onto the soil and plant where they fall. If planting bulbs in grass patches, be sure the areas require no mowing, or is small enough to be trimmed with hand clippers. It is obvious that mowing the grass will also mow down the emerging stalks, so be sure to keep this in mind when thinking of naturalizing bulbs.

BULBS FOR NATURALIZING

Allium	Eranthis	Lilium
Chionodoxa	Fritillaria	Muscari
Colchicums	Galanthus	Narcissus
Crocus	Leucojum	

Depth—Recommended depths at which each species of bulb should be planted are usually included in each package of bulbs. If specific di-

Planting depths for bulb flowers

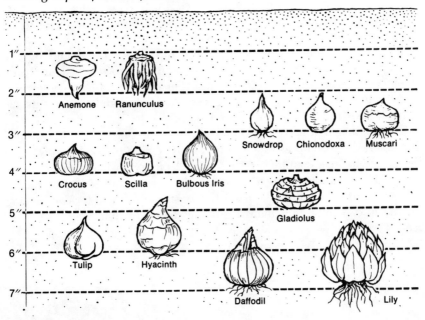

rections are not included, the following suggestions can be used: large bulbs (over two inches in diameter) require a depth of two to three times the diameter of the bulb. Depth measurements of bulbs are taken from the top of the bulb to the normal soil level. Small bulbs (less than two inches in diameter) are planted three to four times their diameter, measured the same way.

Single flower stalks, or even two or three, look lost alone or when used as accent plants. Plant bulbs in groups or clusters, so you achieve a mass effect. The same holds true for color—mass flowers of only one hue and the results will be spectacular. Plant many different colors within the same group and you divide the spectacle and reduce the impact.

BULBS FOR ROCK GARDENS

Allium	Eranthis	Muscari
Anemone	Fritillaria	Narcissus
Camassia	Galanthus	Puschkinia
Chionodoxa	Leucojum	Scilla
Crocus	Lilium	Tulip

Cutting—Almost all bulbs make fine cut flowers for vase display and arrangements, but the cutting must be done correctly or the bulb will be shorn of its ability to store food for succeeding seasons resulting in inferior flowers or no flowers at all.

Cut flowers in the coolest parts of the day, early morning or late afternoon, as soon as the buds open, but not before. To assure beautiful blooms and longer-lasting arrangements, immediately put the stems into cool, clean water and store in a cool, dark part of the house overnight. Arrange the flowers the following morning.

Only bare stemmed flowers—daffodils and amaryllis—should be cut to the ground. All other flowers must be permitted to retain their leaves so they can make the food, to be stored in the bulb, for the following season's growth. Cutting off the leaves along with the flower cuts off your chances for a second season's bloom.

If your blooms are not cut, but remain in the garden for appearance and color, do not clip as long as the petals remain in good shape. Once they start to look shabby, or start to fall off, remove the flower head completely, thereby taking the seed pod off too. All seed pods should be removed to encourage the plant to pay strict attention to food making for the next year, rather than dissipating much of its energy in setting seed.

BULBS FOR CUT FLOWERS

Allium   Hyacinth   Scilla
Anemone   Iris   Tigridia
Dahlia   Lilium   Tritonia
Gladiolus   Muscari   Tulips
Hippeastrum   Narcissus   Zantedeschia

Long stemmed tulips backed by flowering shrub gives unforgettable sight

Digging and Storing Bulbs—Tender bulbs are dug each season and stored until the following spring. Left in the ground all winter, most would be dead by spring. Hardy bulbs can be left in place once planted. However, because they increase and become overcrowded they require lifting, dividing and replanting periodically.

Bulbs are dug after they have flowered and after the leaves have browned and died. Until that time continue watering. On a cool, sunny day, but not on a day after a recent rain has soaked the soil, dig up the bulb, roots, leaves and all. Cut off the tops, check to see that the bulb is not diseased and place in baskets for storage. Hardy bulbs dug to prevent overcrowding can be replanted immediately or else stored in a cool, dry place until autumn planting time. Use mesh bags or baskets with holes for storage, and make sure the storage area is dry with a stable, cool temperature. Tender bulbs are dug, dried in the sun for two days, put into mesh bags and cured at 75° for two or three weeks and then stored in a cool, dark area until spring planting time.

Do not allow bulbs to dry out. Pack them in moist peat moss to store them away. Do not wet or soak the peat moss as this will cause the bulbs to rot—merely dampen it slightly. Gladiolus are an exception to this rule for storage of tender bulbs; they do prefer dry storage, with no moisture added.

Because bulbs fall prey to many insects and some diseases during storage, each bulb should be dusted with an insecticide and a fungicide before planting. Put some insecticide (5% DDT) in a paper bag, drop in a few bulbs, shake gently but thoroughly so the bulb is completely covered with powder, and store the bulbs until planting time.

FALL PLANTED BULBS

Name	Color	Height in Inches	Planting Depth in Inches	Spacing in Inches	Blooms	Requirements	Remarks
Allium		6-36					Onion family member, odor prevails, good for borders, cutting, naturalizing
Odorum	White	20	3	8	August	Full sun-partial shade, well-drained soil	Fine for borders
Chives	Lavender	12	3	6	June		Edible
Karataviense	Pink	8	2	4	June		Leaves better than flowers
Moly	Yellow	12	3	6	June	Partial shade	Fine for arrangements
Anemone (Windflowers)	Blue, white, pink, lavender	6-12					Semi-hardy varieties should be planted in spring, good for rock gardens
Blanda	Lavender	4-6	2	4-6	March	Partial shade, moist soil	Stands bad March weather
Apemnina	Blue	6	2	6	April	Sandy soil	Daisylike flowers
Atrocaerulea	Blue	5	2	5	March	Sandy soil	Folds up on cloudy days
Camassia	Blue, white	18-36					Star-shaped flowers, bloom may wane, so feed well
Esculenta	Blue	20	5	10	May	Moist soil	Plant in clumps
Leichtlinii	Blue	24	5	10	May	Moist soil	Beautiful light blue

173

Fall Planted Bulbs (Continued)

Name	Color	Height in Inches	Planting Depth in Inches	Spacing in Inches	Blooms	Requirements	Remarks
Chionodoxa	Blue	6					Star-shaped flowers face skyward
Luciliae	Blue	6	3	3	March	Sandy soil	Fine in rock gardens, white eye
Sardensis	Blue	6	3	3	March	Sandy soil	No white center
Colchicum (Meadow Saffrons)	Yellow, white, purple	4-12					No leaves when blooming, but large untidy leaves die early, called Autumn crocus
Autumnale	Purple	10	3	6	October	Full sun-partial shade	For rock gardens
Speciosum	Lilac	6	2	6	October		Plant in August
Crocus (Spring flowering, plant in fall)							Harbinger of spring, among best known spring flowers, do not plant in rows
Aureus	Orange	5-6	2-3	3	February	Full sun, sandy, well-drained soil	Good for mass planting
Biflorus	Many	5-6	2-3	3	March	Full sun, well-drained soil	Striped, very hardy
Chrysanthus	White, yellow	5-6	2-3	3	February	Full sun, well-drained soil	Prolific bloomer, large flowers
Sieberi	Lavender	5-6	2-3	3	March	Full sun, sandy, well-drained soil	Very showy
Tomasinianus	Lavender	5-6	2-3	3	March	Full sun, sandy, well-drained soil	Prolific bloomer

Fall Planted Bulbs (*Continued*)

Name	Color	Height in Inches	Planting Depth in Inches	Spacing in Inches	Blooms	Requirements	Remarks
Crocus	(Fall flowering, plant in August)						Flowers come first then foilage, bloom soon after planting
Medius	Lilac	5-6	2-4	3	September	Full sun, sandy, well-drained soil	Showiest autumn crocus
Speciosus	Blue	5-6	2-4	3	October	Full sun, sandy, well-drained soil	Increases freely to mass color
Zonatus	Red-lilac	5-6	2-4	3	September	Full sun, sandy, well-drained soil	Yellow band inside base very showy
Eranthis (Winter Aconite) Cilicica Hyemnalis Tubergenii	Yellow	2-3	2	3-4	February	Well-drained soil	Long-lasting flowers, plant in August-early September
Fritillarias		10-36					One of the prettiest garden flowers, pendulous, large flowers
Imperialis	Orange, yellow, red	36	6-8	12	April	Full sun	Flowers hang from stem with crown of green leaves
Meleagris	White, purple, light purple	16	4	12	April	Partial shade	Drooping bell-shaped flowers

Fall Planted Bulbs (*Continued*)

Name	Color	Height in Inches	Planting Depth in Inches	Spacing in Inches	Blooms	Requirements	Remarks
Galanthus (Snowdrops) Elwesii Nivalis Florepleno Plicatus	White with markings	4-12	3	2-4	February	Full sun-partial shade	Easy to grow, plant in masses, not lines, very early bloomers
Hyacinths	Red, pink, blue, white					Partial shade, rich soil	For formal garden, use exhibition-size bulbs, all others, use smaller bulbs, plant outdoors, September-December, beautiful if forced indoors, many varieties available
Exhibition		10	6-8	6	February-April		
Other		8	6-8	6	April		
Iris							Several hundred varieties (check local nurseryman for specific culture information), just about all colors and combinations available
Dutch	Many	16-24	4	6	May	Full sun, sandy well-drained soil	These three groups are flower shop iris, need protection in winter, semi-hardy, wide color variety
Spanish	Many	16-24	4	4	June		
English	Many	16-24	4	4	July	Full sun, sandy, moist soil	

Fall Planted Bulbs (*Continued*)

Name	Color	Height in Inches	Planting Depth in Inches	Spacing in Inches	Blooms	Requirements	Remarks
Leucojum Aestivum	White	16	4	4	April	Partial shade, well-drained soil	Called snowflakes, for best results do not move after planting
Vernum	White	8	4	4	March		
Lilium (Lilies)	All but blue	1-10 feet	3 times bulb size	Various	May-September	No shade, well-drained, fertile soil	Plant immediately on arrival, do not allow to dry out, many varieties (check local nurseryman for what grows best in your area), many are easy to grow, some should be left to specialists
Muscari (Grape Hyacinth)							
Armeniacum	Blue	6	3	4	March	Full sun-partial shade, well-drained soil	Flowers look like upside-down grape bunches, very free flowering dwarf, good for rock gardens
Botryoides	Blue	6	3	4	April		
Plumosum	Violet	8	3	4	June		
Comosum	Mauve	8-16	3	4	April		
Tubergenianum	Blue	8	3	4			
Narcissus (Includes Daffodils, Jonquils and Narcissi)	Mostly whites and yellows	Various	1-6	3-8	March-May	Full sun-partial shade, well-drained soil	Great many varieties and colors including bicolors, fine for cutting and many other uses, new varieties appear each year in catalogs

Fall Planted Bulbs *(Continued)*

Name	*Color*	*Height in Inches*	*Planting Depth in Inches*	*Spacing in Inches*	*Blooms*	*Requirements*	*Remarks*
Puschkinia Libanotica	Light blue	6	3	3	April	Sandy soil	Very dainty, fine for naturalizing and rock gardens
Libanotica Alba	White	6	3	3	April		
Scilla							Flower profusely despite shade, small bell-shaped flowers
Autumnalis	Lavender	6	3	4	August	Full sun-partial shade, well-drained soil	Naturalize well
Campanulata	Many	12-20	5	4	April		Make good cut flowers
Tubergiana	Light blue with stripes	6	3	4	April		Nice soft blue
Sibirica	Blue	6	3	4	April		One of the best in family
Tulip	Many	12-36	4-6	4-6	March-May	Full sun-partial shade, well-drained soil	Well known and widely planted, best results come when planted in groups of colors that go well together, wide range of colors can clash, many many varieties, usually described by shape or color, check catalogs or local nurseryman for instructions

SPRING PLANTED BULBS

Name	Color	Height in Inches	Planting Depth in Inches	Spacing in Inches	Blooms	Requirements	Remarks
Acidanthera Bicolor Murieliae	White	24-36	4	5	August	Full sun	Similar to gladiolus, nice aroma, plant in April, dig up before ground freezes
Amaryllis	Red, white	24-30	1/3 above in pot		February-May	Full sun, well-drained soil	Because slightest frost kills, usually grown as house plant, huge blooms on sturdy, long stems, leaves come first, die down, then comes flower stack, magnificent flowers
Begonia (Tuberous)	White, red, orange	15-24	2-3	10-15	July	Partial shade, well-drained, rich soil	Beautiful, showy flowers all summer, plant after all danger of frost is past, dig up immediately after first frost, flower types differentiate
Canna	Red, orange, yellow	40-60	2-3	12-18	June	Full sun, moist soil	Magnificent showy flowers, plant after frost is past, dig up after first frost

Spring Planted Bulbs (*Continued*)

Name	Color	Height in Inches	Planting Depth in Inches	Spacing in Inches	Blooms	Requirements	Remarks
Dahlia	Many	12-36	6	18-36	September	Well-drained, moist soil	Incredible number of excellent varieties categorized by size and shape, check with dealer for buying in your locality, different varieties can be used for bedding, borders and almost anything else
Gladiolus	All but blue	24-36	6	8-12	July	Full sun, well-drained soil	Plant every two weeks after danger of frost is gone, flowers open from bottom to top, for all to open after cutting, pinch off top bud after bringing inside
Galtonia (Summer Hyacinth)	White	18-36	6	10-12	August-September	Full sun	Bell-shaped, nicely fragrant flowers
Ismene (Hymenocallis) (Spider Lily)	White, yellow	15-24	4	8-10	June-July	Full sun	Evergreen in warm climates, nice aroma from funnel-like flowers

Spring Planted Bulbs (*Continued*)

Name	Color	Height in Inches	Planting Depth in Inches	Spacing in Inches	Blooms	Requirements	Remarks
Tigridia (Tiger Flower)	Red, white, yellow		3	8	July-August	Full sun, sandy soil	Flowers last only one day, but more appear in rapid succession
Tritonia	White, red, orange	24-36	3	6		Full sun	Magnificent, long-lasting, use as cut flowers
Zantedeschia (Calla Lily) Elliottiana Godefreyana	White, yellow	12-36	6		Winter-spring	Moist, rich soil	In cold climates must be grown in green-house, use for beauti-ful, stately cut flowers

INDOOR FLOWERS FROM FORCED BULBS

Bulbs, both tender and hardy, offer the gardener the possibility of having blooming spring flowers indoors long before they normally bloom outdoors. Forcing, as it is called, consists of raising the temperature and humidity levels considerably over normal levels causing the bulbs to grow and flower. Though it seems most popular with bulbs, forcing is also possible with certain flowering shrubs and several perennials.

BULBS FOR FORCING

Amaryllis	Hyacinths
Crocus	Narcissus
Daffodils	Snowdrops (Galanthus)
Grape Hyacinths (Muscari)	Tulips

Check with a local nurseryman for those varieties best suited for forcing indoors. Buy only these varieties, and buy them in the largest size available. Small or bargain bulbs are usually too small to flower when forced. Place the bulbs into pots or special bulb pans of potting soil (available already mixed) with the top or tip of the bulb just above the soil line. If more than one bulb is placed in a pot, there should be little or no space between the sides of each bulb. Water the soil thoroughly and place the pots outdoors in a garden hole or wooden box and cover with eight to ten inches of sand, moist peat moss, leaves or a combination of all. Do not attempt to store bulbs indoors in a basement. Few normally cool basements ever reach the 40° temperature required to break the bulb's dormancy.

After two or three months "cold" storage, bring the bulbs back inside and keep in a cool (50 to 60°), light (but not direct sunlight), room and water regularly until shoots start to grow. Move the pots into full sunlight, water regularly, keep the temperature at about 65° and wait for your flowers.

Tender bulbs do not need the "cold" storage treatment, so, especially for narcissus, simply place bulbs upright in a shallow pan of sand, pebbles or soil, place in a well-lit room and keep the temperature at no higher than 60°.

Whether you are going to grow flowers from bulbs indoors, outdoors or both, the almost endless number of varieties available practically assures you of beautiful flowers. Though bulbs require a bit more care and attention than certain other flowers, they also give more pleasure than most. The small amount of extra time, money and effort expended on bulbs is repaid manyfold with flowers of unmatched beauty in spring, summer and fall.

CHAPTER 9

Vegetables

Like firm, juicy, rich red tomatoes? Or crisp crunchy lettuce and celery? How about eggplant, zucchini, string beans and green peas? And let's not forget tender, fresh sweet corn, minutes from the stalk, dripping melted butter and bursting with sweetness and flavor.

There is only one place you can get this kind of really good, really fresh, really tasty vegetable—your own home garden. Unless the fruit and vegetable industry suddenly revolutionizes its distribution techniques (which is unlikely) commercial fruits and vegetables will taste just as they do today. The only solution then, is to grow them yourself.

Every home should have a vegetable garden, no matter how small. To get good results, vegetable gardens require care and a considerable amount of work. Better to plant less and care for it more than to plant everything you see in the catalog and then end up having wasted a lot of time, energy and money on mediocre vegetables.

So, start small! Better to regret having made the vegetable garden too small and then decide to enlarge it the following year, than the reverse. Anyway as a new homeowner, your property will demand a great deal of time and attention the first few years, probably far more than you realize.

VEGETABLE-GARDEN LOCATION

Now that you have convinced yourself you still want a vegetable garden (despite all it entails), that the produce from *your* garden will be "out of this world" (even if you do say so yourself), that your garden will be quite small (later to be cut 25 to 30%), your next step is to find a place on your property suitable for growing vegetables.

Many suburban homes are built on lots so small that the choice of garden location can be determined by taking three or four steps in any direction. If, after taking these steps, you don't bump into anything, that's it. For those fortunate enough to have more room, your choice is based upon several important considerations.

Pick a spot that gets sunlight most of the day. This eliminates those areas that are shaded by trees, the house, garage or anything else that blocks off the sun for a substantial part of the day. If only shaded areas are available to you for your vegetable garden, you will get best results by growing only leafy vegetables.

Speaking of trees, do not plant trees or shrubs near your garden or choose a garden site surrounded by them. The competition for water and soil nutrients will be won by the trees and shrubs and your vegetables will be the losers.

Good soil is a prerequisite for a good garden and ultimately for good vegetables. Obviously then, if possible, select an area that has good soil (remember the soil in different parts of your property will vary) and stake your claim in the name of magnificent vegetables. The ideal spot for your vegetable garden is in an area near the back door and within a short hose length of a water faucet. The area should be level, and the soil fertile, well drained, and in unshaded sunlight throughout the day. Be certain too, that you have accounted for the garden in the overall landscaping plan, so it becomes a part of it and adds something to the total picture.

VEGETABLE SELECTION

The mouth watering and colorful names and descriptions found in the seed catalogs cause many of us to succumb to the temptation of selecting one of each kind of vegetable available. This type of selection, one from column A one from column B, may be excellent in a Chinese restaurant, but can be disastrous when planting a garden.

The sensible way to select vegetables and to plan your home garden is based on a few very simple, very obvious and all too often overlooked points:

1) What vegetables do *you* and *your* family really like? Grow only those. If a decision must be made to "cut down" grow only those you *like the best,* and which are especially tasty when home grown.

2) How much room do you have? Often a particular favorite must be eliminated because of lack of space. However, in some cases, such as with sweet corn, the large amount of space required is more than made up by the resulting taste sensation. Carefully plan your vegetable garden so the most economical use is made of each square foot of space. Except in the case of a large family, with many mouths to feed, it is

Pretty-as-a-picture peppers growing in home garden

better to have a little of a lot of things in your vegetable garden than to have a lot of a few things.

3) How much can you eat? Unfortunately, all too often, crops are ready for harvesting all at once. Feast or famine type of thing. Despite the fact that staggered planting will give a somewhat staggered harvest, overplanting of a vegetable is wasteful and unnecessary. Check the accompanying charts to determine the yield of each vegetable, and then plant only as much as you can eat (and/or preserve) and enjoy.

4) Which varieties are best for your area? This is one of the most important considerations and can mean the difference between success and failure. Study the seed catalogs carefully before you buy. Find out if the seed you have in mind will grow well and produce quality vegetables under the conditions prevalent in your area. Remember that each area is different, especially in length of growing season. Don't play long shots and hope that the growing season just might be a little longer this year. Select only those varieties recommended for your area and buy them only from reliable seedsmen.

SELECTED HOME-GROWN VEGETABLES

Vegetable	Recommended Varieties	Sow Seed in Garden	Approximate Days to Harvest	Yield 50 Feet of Row
Asparagus	Mary Washington*, Martha Washington*, Waltham Washington			25 pounds
Bean, green bush	Tender Pod*, Topcrop*, Bountiful	May 15-July 15	50-65	25 quarts
Bean, wax bush	Pencil Pod Wax*, Surecrop Wax*	May 15-July 15	60	25 quarts
Bean, green snap pole	Kentucky Wonder*, Blue Lake	May 15-June 5	65	2 bushels
Bean, bush lima	Fordhook 242*, Triumph	May 15-June 5	75	7 quarts
Bean, lima large-seeded pole	Challenger*, King of the Garden*, Ideal	May 15-June 5	12-14 weeks	10 quarts
Bean, shell	Dwarf Horticultural, French Horticultural	May 15-June 1	60	7 quarts
Beets	Crosby Egyptian (early)*, Detroit Dark Red (late)*	April-August	65	1½ bushels
Broccoli	Calabrese*, Green Sprouting*	March (Flats)#	90	
Brussels Sprouts	Long Island Improved*, Jade	April 15 (Flats)# May	95	

Selected Home-Grown Vegetables *(Continued)*

Vegetable	Recommended Varieties	Sow Seed in Garden	Approximate Days to Harvest	Yield 50 Feet of Row
Cabbage (early)	Golden Acre, Copenhagen Market, Red Acre (Red)	March 1 (Flats)#	70	150 pounds
Cabbage (late)	Danish Ballhead, Wisconsin Hollander	May 15 (Flats)#	110	150 pounds
Cantaloupe	Delicious 51, Iroquois, Harvest Queen	May 15**	80-100	30
Carrots	Tendersweet*, Danver's, Imperator*, Nantes*, Chantaney	April-June	65	1½ bushels
Cauliflower	Early Snowball, Snowball (late)*, Perfection*	March (Flats)#	75-100	
Celery	Summer Pascal (green), Fordhook	March (Flats)# May	140	75 ears
Corn, sweet	North Star, Golden Beauty (early); Golden Bantam, Golden Cross Bantam (mid); Surecross, Honeycross (late); Country Gentlemen (white)	May-June**	75	
Cucumber	Burpee Hybrid, Smoothie, SMR 12 (pickling)	May-June**	54	75 pounds

187

Selected Home-Grown Vegetables (Continued)

Vegetable	Recommended Varieties	Sow Seed in Garden	Approximate Days to Harvest	Yield 50 Feet of Row
Eggplant	New Hampshire Hybrid, Black Beauty	March (Flats)# May-June	75	
Lettuce (head)	Pennlake, Green Lakes, Iceberg	March (Flats)# April	60-80	100 pounds
Lettuce (leaf)	Salad Bowl, Grand Rapids	April on	60-70	50 pounds
Onions, plants	Sweet Spanish, Italian Red		125	1 bushel
Onions, sets	Yellow Globe, Ebenezer		125	1 bushel
Parsley	Moss Curled, Paramount	April-May	120	25 pounds
Peas, early	Little Marvel*, World's Record*, Lincoln*	March-April	58	1 bushel
Peas, late	Thomas Laxton*, Freezonian*	March-April	63	1 bushel
Pepper	California Wonder, Vinedale (early)	March (Flats)#	90	
Potatoes	Irish Cobbler (early), Green Mountains (late)	May	80-100	
Pumpkin	Sugar, Jack O'Lantern	May	90-100	150 pounds
Radish	Cherry Belle, Scarlet Globe (early), Icicle (white)	April on	24	50 bunches

Selected Home-Grown Vegetables (*Continued*)

Vegetable	Recommended Varieties	Sow Seed in Garden	Approximate Days to Harvest	Yield 50 Feet of Row
Spinach	Bloomsdale Long Standing*, America, Virginia Savoy (fall)*	April-July	36	1 bushel
Squash, summer	Zucchini, Caserta, Yankee Hybrid, Early Prolific	May-June	50-65	75 pounds
Squash, winter	Butternut*, Buttercup*, Delicious, Acorn	May-June	110	100 pounds
Tomatoes, red	Moreton Hybrid, Rutgers, Marglobe, Big Boy	March (Flats)#	70-80	175 pounds
Tomatoes, yellow	Sunray, Golden Jubilee	March (Flats)#	70-80	
Watermelon (icebox)	Sugar Baby, N.H. Hybrid (icebox), R.I. Red (large)	April 15 (Flats)# May 10	70-85	200 pounds

* Freeze well.
** Plant in hills, several plants to a hill.
\# Sow seed indoors in flats where marked, others sow outdoors in garden.

189

SOIL PREPARATION

To hear the "green thumbers" tell it, all you have to do is stick a few seeds in the ground and the results will be the biggest and the best. It takes a lot more than that. However, the procedures are not complicated and fortunately, nature often overlooks many of our more foolish mistakes. But, the inexperienced gardener should realize that these procedures are meant to be followed and, as closely as possible for best results.

New and old gardeners have the same task each spring as they prepare to plant vegetables—the soil must be made ready to accept and nourish the seed or seedlings. The only advantage the established gardener has is an established garden—his soil will be that much richer from having been fertilized and nourished year after year. Soil preparation consists of conditioning the soil so it is neither hard and crusty when dry, nor gummy when wet, checking and regulating acidity, and adding fertilizer and organic matter as required.

Plowing and Conditioning—The idea is to get the garden area dug up and ready for conditioning. Depending upon who is doing the describing it can be called plowing, tilling, spading, turning over, or turning under. Turning the soil by hand is only feasible for the very small area. Using a spade or fork, dig down about six to eight inches. Lift out the soil clod, turn it over and drop back into place. Continue until the entire area is turned and you are convinced this whole vegetable garden is a big mistake. Rake smooth, and then you are ready for the next step.

With motorized equipment, (a tiller or tiller attachment to a power handle) the job is considerably easier. If you expect to have a garden of some size every year, this is a consideration when deciding on the type of power equipment you will buy. Be especially careful when using a tiller, as well as any other power equipment. They are not toys and can cause serious injury if used improperly. Pay strict attention to what you are doing and what the equipment is doing, at all times. Wear proper clothing, sturdy work pants and good heavy shoes, and never, never put your hands near the blades of the tiller while it is running. With most tillers the depth of cut is regulated by the size of the blades and the fineness is regulated by the speed at which you walk behind the unit—the slower you walk the finer the soil will be when you are finished tilling.

Plowing can be done in either spring or fall. If done in the fall just turn or till, do not rake smooth. Spring plowing should be done just before you are ready to sow your seed, so you plow, rake and seed in

Soil must be of good tilth for growing tasty vegetables

reasonably rapid order. Do not attempt to turn over the soil if it is too wet, it will become compacted and defeat your purpose. Check by crumbling a handful of soil between your fingers—if it crumbles and does not feel sticky, it is ready for plowing.

Correct Soil Acidity—Most vegetables grow best in a soil that is slightly acid. Check your soil or have it checked at a nursery or county agricultural station, and apply additives to bring it either down or up to the proper acidity level. If your soil is more acid than it should be for growing vegetables, add lime, but don't overlime. Soil that is even a bit more acid than recommended is better left alone. Alkaline soils can be made to have a higher acid level by applying proper amounts of either aluminum sulphate or sulphur to the soil. At the time you have the soil tested the tester will indicate the correct amounts of either lime or sulphur to correct any deficiency. Either the lime or the sulphur, according to your soil requirements, can be worked into the soil at the same time you fertilize.

Fertilizing—Most gardens require the addition of fertilizer whether or not they have been previously worked. A check of your soil, made at the same time the acid level is determined, will reveal the proper amounts of nitrogen, phosphoric acid and potash required to bring your soil to the desired level. Organic matter added to the soil does much to enrich the soil and give it a better consistency for planting. These materials (such as manure or vegetable wastes) should not be used in place of chemical fertilizers, but as a supplement to them.

There are two ways to add fertilizer to the soil, both of which give equally good results. Just before you turn over the soil in the fall, spread the correct amount of fertilizer, along with any other additives that your soil requires, and spade or plow under. This method mixes everything together and allows the chemicals to become a part of the soil in the period between the plowing and the planting. In the other method, the soil is plowed and allowed to stand fallow until planting time. Then the fertilizer is spread over only the area to be planted and raked into the top four inches of soil. Each area is fertilized and raked immediately prior to planting.

Vegetable gardens require several fertilizing sessions for best results. The first application is in the spring or fall before plowing, or just before raking and planting. If you are starting your vegetable plants from seedlings, the second fertilizing comes at the time the seedlings are transplanted to the garden. Use a mixture of soluble fertilizer and water as a starter and pour around the roots of the seedlings according to the directions on the fertilizer package. This starter solution will help ease the shock of transplanting and also give the seedlings an added boost to a fast, successful start.

An additional shot of fertilizer is given to the plants once they are growing and well established, and this is done on the basis of the kind of vegetable. For example, when leafy vegetables, root crops and greens are about half grown, apply a ring of fertilizer to the soil about four inches from the stem of the plant, work gently into the soil with a hoe or cultivator, and water well. A similar sidedressing of fertilizer should be applied to plants that set fruit, like peppers, tomatoes, cucumbers and corn, just as the plants begin to set these fruits. Be especially careful about working the fertilizer into the soil. Deep cultivation may damage shallow roots and do more harm than the fertilizer will do good.

SOWING SEEDS

Vegetable seeds when given the proper environment, will germinate, become sturdy seedlings and develop into healthy, bearing plants. The trick is to do the planting correctly and, happily, the trick is not a difficult one.

Timing is of the utmost importance when planting vegetable seeds or putting out seedlings. Divided into two major groups, cool-season crops and warm-season crops, vegetable seeds must be planted during that time of year when germination is most probable for the specific kind of vegetable. For example, the cool-season crops such as lettuce, cabbage, onions, celery, spinach and other root vegetables grow best when temperature is in the 50's, and at this temperature, germination is greatest too.

The warm-season crops, tomatoes, eggplant, corn, cucumbers, squash and all melons, grow and germinate best at temperatures in the upper 60's. This does not imply that seed will not germinate at temperatures other than those recommended. Though some vegetables will germinate at widely divergent temperatures, the result is weak, spindly plants at the higher level temperatures, and less germination and more rotted

Corn planted between rows of plastic mulch. Grass clippings keep weeds down between stalks

seeds at the lower level temperatures. Check the accompanying tables and match with your own local conditions and "last frost date" maps for the correct time to sow vegetable seeds. The same timing considerations apply to transplanting seedlings as to sowing directly into the ground. To have seedlings ready for transplanting, sow the seed into flats indoors or into a cold frame about six to eight weeks before they are supposed to be planted outdoors in the garden.

HOME GROWN VEGETABLES PLANTING DATA

Vegetable	Distance between rows in inches	Seed or plants for 50 feet of row	Planting Depth in inches	Distances between plants in inches
Asparagus	48		8	18
Bean, green bush	24	½ pound	1½	4
Bean, wax bush	24	½ pound	1½	4
Bean, green snap pole	30	½ pound	1½	4-6 per pole
Bean, bush lima	30	½ pound	1½	4-6
Bean, lima large seeded pole	36	½ pound	1½	4-6 per pole
Bean, shell	30	½ pound	1½	4
Beets	18	½ ounce	1	3
Broccoli	30	25 plants		18
Brussels Sprouts	30	25 plants		18
Cabbage (early)	30	25 plants		18
Cabbage (late)	30	25 plants		18
Cantaloupe	60	1 packet	½	48
Carrots	18	½ ounce	½	2
Cauliflower	30	25 plants		18
Celery	24	100		6
Corn, sweet	36	¼ pound	1½	24 (hills)

Home Grown Vegetables Planting Data *(Continued)*

Vegetable	Distance between rows in inches	Seed or plants for 50 feet of row	Planting Depth in inches	Distances between plants in inches
Cucumber	60**	1 packet	1	48
Eggplant	30	1 packet	1	24
Lettuce (head)	18	1 packet	¼	12
Lettuce (leaf)	18	1 packet	¼	12
Onions, plants	18	150 plants		4
Onions, sets	18	1 pound		4
Parsley	18	1 packet	¼	6
Peas, early	24	½ pound	1	2
Peas, late	30	½ pound	1	2
Pepper	24-30	20 plants		20
Potatoes	30	3 pounds	3	8
Pumpkin	96	½ ounce	1	96
Radish	12	1 packet	½	2
Rhubarb	36	use plants		36
Spinach	12	½ ounce	½	4
Squash, summer	36**	1 packet	1	36
Squash, winter	60**	1 packet	1	60
Tomatoes, red	48	1 packet	¼	36
Tomatoes, yellow	48	1 packet	¼	36
Watermelon (icebox)	72	8 or 9 seeds		36

* Freezes well.
** Plant in hills, several plants to a hill.
\# Sow seed indoors in flats where marked others sow outdoors in garden.

Outdoor—The ABC's of vegetable seed sowing are simple and so easily followed that there is no reason why they should not be followed to a "T":

a) Use only fresh, known-brand seed. Seed is quite inexpensive, so it doesn't pay to economize and then be sorry about the number or the quality of plants produced.

b) Plant all seeds in light, well-cultivated, well-fertilized soil. Be certain the soil is in the best condition possible to receive the seeds.

c) Double check your planting plan to be certain that all vegetables will be in areas best suited to their growth and that enough room has been allocated for their mature size. See, for example, that corn stalks do not shadow low-growing vegetables and that vines such as melons and cucumbers will not overrun neighboring vegetables.

d) Plant in straight rows, marked off by taut string. The straighter the rows are made, the easier will be weed control, insect control and even harvesting.

e) Make shallow furrows for small seed and slightly deeper furrows for larger seed. A rule of thumb for seed planting is to plant seeds four times as deep as the size of the seed. Make shallow furrows with a broom or hoe handle drawn along your marking string. Deeper furrows are made with the corner of a hoe blade. The charts in this chapter indicate the recommended planting depth for most vegetables.

f) Place the seed according to directions. Some seed is placed in hills, others in drills. Corn and melon seed is hilled (several seeds are placed in a single spot at regular intervals down the row). Most other seeds, especially the very small ones are drilled (spaced by hand evenly all along the row).

g) Be sure seeds are spaced properly according to the seed chart in the book, or the package directions. The chart shows final spacing, that is, after thinning out. Package directions are usually given before thinning, with instructions to thin out seedlings to a final spacing.

h) Cover the newly planted seed with the dirt that was piled up on either side of the furrow when the furrow was made. Tamp gently, but do not pack down. Small seedlings cannot fight their way through tightly packed down soil.

i) Water thoroughly but do not drown. Keep the seeded area moist, but not wet, until germination, then water as required.

Indoor—There are several reasons to sow seed indoors to make seedlings that will be transplanted to the garden at a later date. Among the best reasons are; it allows the amateur to get started despite the snow on the ground, it lengthens the growing season, allowing slower-growing vegetables to mature fully thanks to the early head start, and the ability to grow good, healthy plants of delicate varieties like celery which cannot be started from seed sown directly into the ground. To start seed indoors:

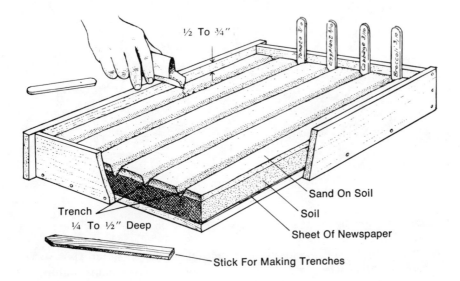

Efficient and economical way to plant seeds for seedlings

a) Select a container of the correct size. Many different kinds are available including peat pots, fiberboard flats, plastic pots, seed flats and plant bands. Try each and decide which you prefer for next year's planting.

b) Use a mixture of fine sand and sphagnum peat moss, vermiculite or specially prepared "seed-starting soil." Fill the container about halfway with the soil.

c) Water the soil thoroughly and allow it to stand so excess water drains off.

d) Make furrows in the wet soil with a small stick, dowel or pencil. Have the furrow run the long way down the container.

e) Sow seed lightly and evenly in the furrow. The better spaced the seeds are, the better the chance for useful, healthy seedlings.

f) Cover the seed with a thin layer of the same type of soil that was used in the container.

g) Water the top layer of soil, but be very gentle so the seed is not washed away. If possible, use a mist sprayer and cover the soil with a heavy mist of water.

h) Encase the entire container in a plastic bag or sheet plastic of the type that comes from clothes cleaning shops. The plastic holds in moisture and softens the light, promoting better, fuller germination.

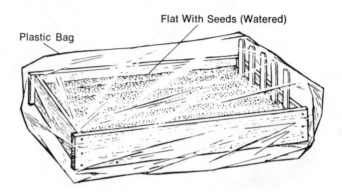

Plastic Bag

Flat With Seeds (Watered)

Plastic bag keeps moisture in and speeds germination

i) Place the plastic enclosed container in a warm, sunlit spot until germination takes place. Be sure the spot selected remains uniformly warm and has soft sunlight for at least six hours each day.

Dibble is used to "pop-out" seedlings   *Also helps in replanting seedlings*

j) Do nothing else to the flat until after the first *true* leaves have appeared. Then open the plastic bag and transplant the seedlings to larger containers, pots or flats, such as individual peat pots.

Since seedlings will become stringy and weak if kept in a sunny window for the entire period between germination and transplanting into the open garden, be prepared to put the seedlings into a cold frame or hot bed for a short time. If this is impossible, don't grow your own seedlings, buy them from a local nurseryman. Most varieties are available at the large nurseries and garden shops, and though they are more expensive and less fun than "doing it yourself," sometimes you have no choice.

TRANSPLANTING SEEDLINGS

Vegetables most often started in the garden as seedlings are; lettuce, celery, cabbage, tomatoes, eggplant, broccoli and peppers. Others that are usually available as transplants for early starting include melons, cucumbers, many herbs and cauliflower. For best results when transplanting seedlings:

a) Select only the sturdiest seedlings for transplanting—they have the best chance of survival. Be sure that the seedlings have been "hardened off" or toughened by withholding water and lowering the temperature in the cold frame or hot bed for seven to ten days prior to transplanting.

b) Approximately ten days before transplanting, block or cut the roots of each plant in the flat. A sharp knife is used to cut through the soil in the flat of seedlings, forming cubes of soil and roots. Try to include as much soil and as many roots as possible with each transplant. Individually peat potted seedlings need not be blocked, but can be transplanted pot and all. Seedlings bought from a nursery

Cubed seedling comes with roots intact in block of soil

should be cut into cubes just before transplanting, and here too, include as much soil and roots as possible with each transplant.

c) Once the seedling has been blocked, plant immediately. If this suddenly becomes impossible (heavy rain, unexpected company, etc.) be sure to keep the seedlings, the earth, and the roots moist until they are transplanted into the garden.

d) Do all seedling transplanting on cloudy days or after the sun has gone down. The hot, daytime sun takes its toll of delicate seedlings.

e) Dig holes that are large enough to accommodate the seedlings with their earth ball and roots intact. Since the seedlings should be planted slightly deeper than previously, allow for this when making the hole. For many of the blocked-off seedlings, a tulip bulb planter makes a hole just the right size.

f) Place a small handful of composted material in the bottom of the hole and then carefully place the seedling in the hole.

g) Water with a starter solution made of diluted liquid fertilizer and water, or a solution made of one-half pound of 5-10-5 fertilizer dissolved in four gallons of water. Water thoroughly but do not drown the plants.

h) Replace the soil in the hole, working it in with your fingers so no air spaces remain around the roots. Do not pack solid, but tamp firmly.

i) If, immediately upon completing the transplanting, you have any doubts about the weather, either too hot or too cold, protect the seedlings with hotcaps, baskets or other covers. Remove the protectors as quickly as possible after the weather has settled and the seedlings are established.

WEED PREVENTION AND CONTROL

If your soil is well fertilized and capable of producing the largest and best vegetables in the area, it is also capable of producing some immense weeds. Because weeds are neither what you planted nor what you want to grow, don't admire their size and strength, get rid of them. Not only are they unsightly but, more important, they steal nutrients and water from the vegetables you did plant and do want. Select one of the following methods to prevent, kill and control garden weeds.

Cultivation—Though the word conjures up visions of huge tractors and mechanized cultivation equipment, the home gardener will become much more familiar with a far different kind of cultivator. This is the kind carried around in the hand, while crawling around on hands and knees down the rows and around the plants. Long-handled cultivators are also available for those who prefer an upright position. The hoe or cultivator is used to break up the soil and uproot weeds, leaving the area around the vegetables loose and relatively weed free. Be very

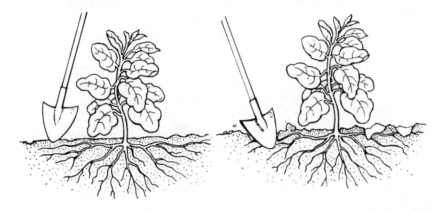

Cultivate lightly (left) or tool will cut through roots (right)

careful when weeding though, as a single misguided swing with a hoe can cut a tomato or other plant in half. Below-surface cultivation can also damage and even sever vegetable plant roots that are close to the surface. Start cultivation as soon as, or a few days before weeds appear and continue throughout the growing season on an "as required" schedule.

Mulching—A sort of preventive measure, mulching consists of covering the soil around plants with a protective material, usually one which is in easy supply, to block out weeds. As an added bonus, mulches also keep moisture in the soil, regulate and maintain soil temperature and keep vegetables like tomatoes and cucumbers clean and out of contact with the soil. Some good mulches are grass clippings, peat moss, cocoa husks, ground corncobs, straw, leaves and black plastic.

Best results are obtained if mulches are put down as soon as the plant is well established. The exception is black plastic which is put into position first and the plants then set into holes punctured in the plastic. Water the area to be mulched thoroughly, before placing the organic material. Then put down the mulch, and water again. Be generous with the mulching material but, as with many other things, don't be overgenerous. Leaves or straw are put down about four-inches thick and mulches like peat moss or other thick mulches go down in a two-inch depth. A too thick mulch can be harmful because it absorbs light rains before they hit the soil.

If considerable amounts of organic material are used as mulches throughout the growing season, they should be left in the garden to help condition the soil when plowed under. To avoid a lack of nitrogen in the soil caused by the various bacteria competing for the available nitrogen, add a considerable quantity of nitrogen-high fertilizer to the soil and mulch, just prior to turning under in the fall.

Chemicals—Several companies have developed chemical weed killers for the vegetable garden. They cannot be recommended to the new gardener since their use is a bit tricky. Because these compounds are herbicides, a slight error or chance breeze can cause the chemicals to fall or drift onto vegetables and plants resulting in considerable damage. If you decide to use chemical weed killers in your vegetable garden, read all the directions thoroughly, follow them to the letter and let extreme caution be your byword.

WATERING

If you are really interested in top quality vegetables, be prepared to supply them with the water they need to grow. For maximum plant growth and luscious vegetables, an inch of rainfall each week is required. This means if there is little or no rain during extended periods, *you* must supply the water.

Though it is true that a little water is better than no water at all, frequent light waterings do little good, if any. Therefore, water your garden according to the following recommendations.

Water at least once a week when rainfall has been limited or light.

Vegetable garden in black plastic and grass clipping mulches

Bubbler watering head is especially good for vegetable gardens

To determine both the amount of rainfall and the amount of your own watering, place coffee cans at several spots in the garden. Measuring the amount of water in the cans after a rain or watering will tell you how much water has hit the soil. To be certain, water once a week for long enough to accumulate at least one inch of water. As a guide, it takes approximately 600 gallons to supply an inch of water to a garden 20 x 50 feet. If your sprinkler or timer has a measuring device, you can set it at the length of time required to drop this 600 gallons of water for every one thousand square feet of garden.

Always water during that part of the day that will see the water doing the most good for your plants. Watering during the hottest part of the day will result in considerable evaporation, so avoid it. Also water enough before sundown so the leaves have time to dry off. This will prevent certain fungi and other diseases from getting a start.

INSECT AND DISEASE CONTROL

Insects and diseases have as much interest in your magnificent vegetables as you do. A regular program of spraying with an all-purpose compound should protect your interest. Start spraying as soon as recommended by the chemical manufacturer. Certain insects may get through this pro-

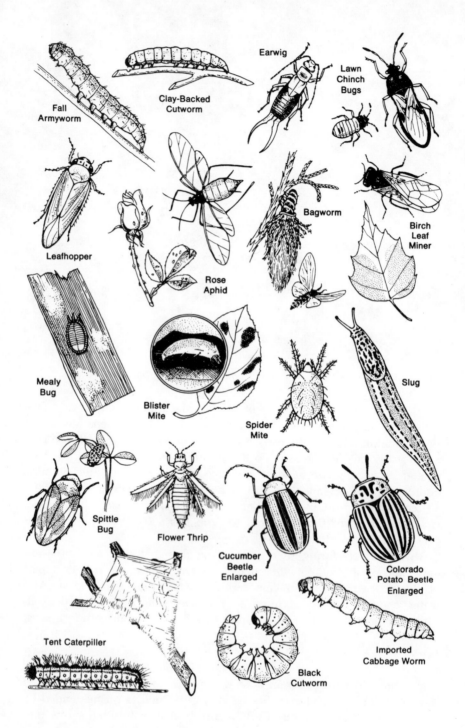

Fall Armyworm

Clay-Backed Cutworm

Earwig

Lawn Chinch Bugs

Leafhopper

Rose Aphid

Bagworm

Birch Leaf Miner

Mealy Bug

Blister Mite

Spider Mite

Slug

Spittle Bug

Flower Thrip

Cucumber Beetle Enlarged

Colorado Potato Beetle Enlarged

Tent Caterpiller

Black Cutworm

Imported Cabbage Worm

Tomato hornworm can eat through and ruin entire plant in about 2 days

tective shield, so be prepared with specialized insecticides and use as directed. Be careful that directions are followed concerning the number of days between spraying and harvesting. Wash everything that comes from the garden very carefully before eating. Don't get so carried away by the beauty of your vegetables that you pick a tomato or pepper and eat it while standing in the garden. Spray residue will not only ruin the taste of the vegetable, but might ruin you too.

HARVESTING

If you have weathered all the storms and pitfalls that go into successful vegetable gardening, your reward comes at harvest time. However, sometimes it's hard to know just when that time is. All your vegetables do not mature at the same time, and often leaving them just one extra day can mean the difference between the peak of flavor and overripe vegetables. The following suggestions give you some idea as to when and how to get the best possible crop from your garden:

ASPARAGUS should not be cut for the first two years. The third year, cut all stalks for a period of about one month, and leave uncut the second month. Asparagus that are at least four years old may be cut clean for a two month period, and then allowed to store food for the next year's growth.

BEANS should be picked at their peak of flavor—when they are young and tender. Pick often and the plant will continue to produce beans for a longer period than if you harvest only once or twice. Beans should not be fat. Don't think that the bigger and fatter they are, the better they will taste. The young, thin beans taste the sweetest.

BEETS are pulled when they are between one and one-half to three inches in diameter, according to variety. Use as quickly as possible after pulling, or keep in a cool moist area until ready to be cooked and eaten.

BROCCOLI is cut in the morning when it looks just like green cauliflower. If it is taken with about six inches of stem just before the heads start to separate, broccoli will continue to bear from other shoots that will appear after the first head has been cut.

BRUSSELS SPROUTS buds are broken off when they are between one and one and one-half inches in diameter. Keep cool until cooked.

CABBAGE heads are cut when they are firm, but don't allow the heads to get too big or they will split. Trim off coarse outer leaves before refrigerating.

CANTALOUPE must be harvested at exactly the correct time to insure peak flavor. Pick melons when the stems separate from the fruit with only a slight pull. Don't try to smell melons as shoppers do in super markets. It will probably tell you nothing and you'll look ridiculous crawling around smelling melons. Rely on the easily pulled stem test.

CARROTS are pulled when young and crisp and used as soon as possible. Successive sowings should give continuous harvest.

CAULIFLOWER leaves should be tied over the head as it forms to blanche vegetable white. Cut about two to three weeks after heads have been covered with leaves. Make sure head is firm before cutting.

CELERY, whether eaten green or blanched white by holding light from stalks with coverings, is harvested by cutting the stalk about three inches below ground.

CORN is picked when the silks are brown and the kernels milky. Clean outdoors and race into kitchen. Dump immediately into boiling water. Top with melted butter. One bite and all the work and time spent in the garden will be repaid to you one hundred fold.

CUCUMBERS should not be allowed to get too large or yellow. Keep checking daily, looking carefully under the leaves for newly matured fruits. Ripe cucumbers appear suddenly sometimes, especially after a heavy rain.

EGGPLANT is cut from stem with a knife or garden clippers. Pick when skin is dark and shiny and about 4 inches in diameter.

LETTUCE comes in two forms—leaf and head. Leaf lettuce is harvested as often as leaves are of eating size. Head lettuce should be cut as soon as full and round, Heat will ruin good lettuce so don't wait too long to harvest.

ONIONS are ready when tops look dead. Dig up and allow them to remain in the sun for a few days so skins can become tough. This is especially important if onions are to be stored.

PARSLEY is picked as required but allow some leaves to remain so growth continues.

PEAS are picked when small, sweet and tender. If they get too big they become tough. Pick only during cool parts of the day, never in very hot sun.

PEPPERS are picked when firm, full sized and just before they turn red.

POTATOES are dug up after vines have begun to die. Skins will toughen for better storing if potatoes are allowed to remain on the ground in the sun for a full day.

PUMPKINS are pulled when mature, but do not allow them to become overlarge.

RADISHES are pulled quickly when mature. If you wait a little too long, they become woody.

RHUBARB stalks should not be cut, pull when harvesting. Second year harvest lightly, but from third year on a heavy harvest is okay, and will not hurt roots.

SPINACH tops should be broken when they are 4-inches long and new shoots will follow until the first frost. Cool-season types are harvested only once by cutting individual plants.

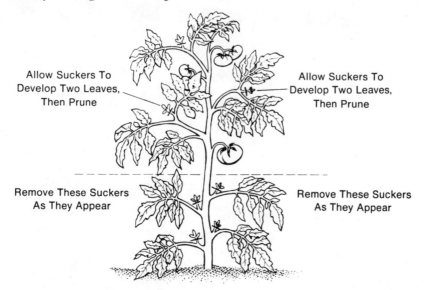

Allow Suckers To Develop Two Leaves, Then Prune

Allow Suckers To Develop Two Leaves, Then Prune

Remove These Suckers As They Appear

Remove These Suckers As They Appear

Remove all suckers from tomato plants after they develop two leaves

SQUASH fruit is cut from stems before skin hardens. Pick fruit as soon as ready, for vines stop growing when ripe fruit is allowed to remain on vine.

TOMATOES are picked when fully ripe and firm to the touch. Do not allow to become soft and overripe. There is nothing like a sweet, ripe tomato—it makes all the time, money and effort spent on a vegetable garden worth it.

Stake tomato plant with loose loop of cord or plastic-covered wire

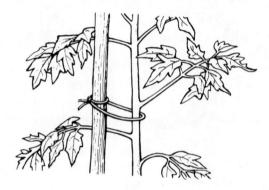

CHAPTER 10

Insects, Diseases and Their Control

Most aspects of gardening tend toward the positive, or more accurately, the superlative, as people strive for bigger, better, prettier, etc., plants. Unfortunately, as in life, gardening is not all sweetness and light. It always seems that just as flowers, vegetables and trees reach their peak, they are attacked by all manner of pests—insects, diseases, funguses, birds, animals and even children. The tempting solution is simply to throw up one's hands in disgust and give up. But, how many of us could really forget all the dollars spent, the hours of labor and the tender loving care we lavished upon these plants. Give up without a fight? Never!

Actually, the fight is not really even a fight, but rather a routine of good garden practices. The routine goes something like; prevention, determination, and remedy.

INSECT AND DISEASE PREVENTION

It stands to reason that the better you make your prevention program, the easier will be the task of keeping your plants healthy. However, most new gardeners do little in the way of preventing insects and disease, preferring to stack all their hopes and labors on the chemical killers so widely available today. While it is true that most home gardens require some help in disease and insect control from the man-made chemicals, gardeners should investigate the following suggestions for good garden practice, and relegate the use of "cides" to emergency or overwhelming situations.

1. Buy only from recognized nurserymen and only those plants certified to be disease free.

2. Select plants from the list of immune or resistant varieties. Each year new varieties are added to the list.
3. Keep plants healthy with the proper amounts of water and fertilizer. Too much of either can cause as much trouble as too little.
4. Maintain garden areas so they are weed free.
5. Keep gardens and planting beds clean. Do not allow garden wastes, sick or diseased plant parts or other debris to remain among healthy plants.
6. Keep beds mulched with clean mulch. Mulch that is neither clean nor weed free can cause considerable trouble.
7. Practice crop rotation in even the smallest gardens. Many diseases and pests that remain in the soil can be successfully combated by moving the plants around within the garden. In other words, if tomatoes are on the left one year, plant them on the right of the garden the next year, and so on. Of course, permanent plantings such as trees and shrubs cannot be moved, but for those plants that can be moved, the trip will benefit all but the insects and pests.
8. Investigate the natural enemies of damage causing insects, and strive to keep them doing their job in and around your garden. Included in these natural enemies are other insects and birds.
9. Check your garden regularly, looking specifically for insects or diseases that have attacked your plants when you were not watching. Regular inspections can save many plants from total destruction.
10. Destroy any insect ridden or diseased portions of plants as quickly as possible. On trees and shrubs carefully paint the pruned area with tree-wound paint to discourage insects from entering the open wound.
11. Determine the cause of any trouble as quickly as possible and deal with it immediately.

FINDING THE CAUSE OF PLANT DAMAGE

Most insects and diseases are relatively easy to spot by the kind of damage left in their wake. Anything out of the ordinary should be checked and, if identification is difficult, take a portion of the damaged plant to a local nurseryman or state extension service for positive identification.

Check both upper and underside of all leaves for tell-tale damage from insects and diseases. Most insects are either chewers or suckers—chewers actually leave holes in leaves or around the edges, suckers cause the plant to take on an unhealthy looking yellow-green color. Any time plants look less than vigorous and healthy, start looking for a cause. Correct identification of the trouble will lead you to a cure much more quickly than a shotgun approach of spraying everything in sight in the hope that it will take care of all possible problems.

INSECTICIDES, FUNGICIDES, MITICIDES, ETC.

Clear, simple, easy-to-follow directions come with each chemical preparation, be it herbicide, miticide, fungicide or insecticide, and these directions are meant to be followed exactly. Too little of a chemical cuts the strength and makes it useless against certain insects or diseases, while too much of the same chemical can cause permanent injury to certain plants. The following checklist indicates the recommended steps for safe, effective use of all garden chemicals.

1. Buy only what you need, and use what you buy. Don't buy "one of each" so you can be prepared for any eventuality while impressing your neighbors with your collection. Use your sprays and dusts in a regular program of preventive spraying. A thorough, effective protection program can eliminate a large percentage of garden problems.

2. If you have not sprayed preventively, or for one reason or another pests and diseases are attacking your plants, try to identify the problem and then treat it. General purpose mixtures are available and can be used successfully to control many insects and diseases of plants. However, in most cases, specific chemicals formulated for specific problems do a better, less expensive job.

3. Check into the various kinds of sprays available, and again, buy according to the problem at hand. For example, the three basic kinds of pesticides: stomach poisons, contact poisons and fumigants, are manufactured to be effective against specific pests. Use the right chemical, and use it where it will do the most good.

4. Investigate the relatively new systemic chemicals that are absorbed into the plant and protect from within. Especially effective in areas with considerable rainy weather, systemics, once absorbed cannot wash off. They remain effective, no matter what kind of weather, for up to about two weeks. Obviously, using systemics on edible plants and produce make them poisonous to humans and pets. So never use systemics on vegetables, fruits, or anything else that is to be eaten. Systemics should be carefully controlled during spraying because they can be absorbed through the skin of humans.

5. Carefully read the directions each time a garden chemical is used, and follow the directions exactly. Pay particular attention to the "caution" area on the label and follow all precautionary instructions rigidly.

6. Keep all garden chemicals out of the reach of children and pets.

The best place for these chemicals is in a locked cabinet or closet. If locking them up is impossible, they should surely be placed on a very high shelf.

7. Use only clean spray equipment. Clean out sprayers after each use by washing thoroughly in detergent and rinsing in clear water several times. Never leave chemicals in the spray equipment until "next time". This will surely ruin your spray equipment, and dilute the power of the chemical as well.

8. Obviously then, use only fresh chemicals, and except in rare cases when it is indicated on the label, do not save chemicals from one season to the next. Buy fresh chemicals as you need them and get rid of the unused portion at the end of the season.

9. Never "borrow" measuring spoons or cups from the kitchen for use with garden chemicals. If needed desperately and borrowed, they should never be returned.

10. Consider the weather before you spray, and spray only on days when you have complete control over the chemicals. Never spray on a windy day. Drifting sprays can land on nearby plants and cause great damage. Also, if rain is forecast, don't spray as you will have to repeat immediately after the rain washes the plants clean.

11. Spray carefully so you cover all parts of the plant; top and bottom of leaves, soil around trunk, and the trunk and limbs. Cover thoroughly but do not soak. No dripping means poor coverage, too much dripping means wasted chemicals, so find the happy medium.

12. Hand pick and destroy any insects that are large enough.

13. Mix a commercially prepared spreader sticker solution with garden chemicals to give them better adhesive qualities. If none is available, a tablespoon of laundry detergent for each gallon of spray will do the job.

14. Check and double check the instructions and mixing amounts before spraying. Check also to be sure that the particular type of plant on which you plan to use this spray will not be harmed by the ingredients in the spray you have selected.

15. Never use the same sprayer for poisons (herbicides) as you use for other sprays, no matter how thoroughly you wash it between use. Even the slightest residues left by the herbicide can cause considerable damage to plants. Keep two separate sprayers, and label them clearly.

SPRAY AND DUST APPLICATION EQUIPMENT

Spraying and dusting equipment runs the gamut from less-than-a-dollar "flit gun" types to huge motorized units costing several hundred dollars. The new homeowner is better off going to neither extreme, buying instead a sprayer best suited to the property size and number of plants to be sprayed.

Sprayers and dusters each have their respective devotees, and the only one who can decide for you is you. Generally speaking, it is easier and quicker to dust, however, only on a near windless day. Although sprayers require a bit more mixing and messing, they can be used on slightly windy days, and can project the chemical much farther (like the tops of trees) than a duster.

For the gardeners selecting dusters, both the hand models with pump action and the rotary dusters do an effective job. Before actually buying this piece of equipment, look around and see the advantages and disadvantages of several different models. Try to look for one which has a long extension tube (so you don't have to keep bending over to dust low plants, etc.) and which has a dust nozzle designed to provide an even amount of dust all the way across the mouth. When using your duster, position it so the dust comes out in an upward direction—this will get dust on the underside of the leaves and adequately cover the tops of the leaves with the dust that settles downward.

Among the many different kinds of sprayers available, the best types for the small garden are the compressed air sprayers, hose end, or trombone sprayers. Compressed air sprayers are very popular for small properties and a single loading will usually take care of all requirements. However, most of these require frequent pumping and the metal ones are quite heavy when filled with the liquid chemical solution. The new plastic models now available are much lighter, and should be carefully considered if the spraying is to be done by a woman. Also, remember to shake the sprayer often while in use; they have no built-in agitators, and without shaking, the chemicals can become separated from the solution. You will then end up spraying your plants with pure water, and leaving all the chemicals at the bottom of the sprayer.

Hose-end sprayers are very easy to use, but are limited in that they can only reach as far as your hose can reach. Also, thorough coverage and accurate chemical dilution is only possible, with these sprayers, where the water power is sufficient and constant and when the diluting mechanism is kept very clean.

Trombone sprayers use a pail for their supply of chemical solution and can reach the tops of most trees. Although not as fancy as other sprayers, these simple two-handed units are very effective when in operation.

Whichever type of sprayer or duster you choose, be sure it will do your specific job; the whole job, before you buy it.

INSECT AND DISEASE IDENTIFICATION

Unless you know what you are fighting, the odds of your winning are very slim. The following charts list the most frequent plant pests and diseases and how to combat them. If your problem defies identification, samples sent to your county agent or nurseryman should supply the answer along with the best possible remedy.

LAWN DISEASES AND THEIR CONTROL

Disease	Damage	Cause	Control
Brown Patch	Irregular light brown patches of grass, may have purple "halo" in morning	Fungus—thrives in hot, humid weather	Water lawn only in morning, use Dyrene or Ortho lawn & turf fungicide
Fairy Rings	Dark green circles surrounding dead grass, sometimes produces mushrooms	Many funguses	Make holes around circumference, pour in fungicide or fumigate soil with Methyl Bromide
Dollar Spot	Brown patches of grass about size of silver dollar	Fungus—at its worst in cool, wet weather	Same as Brown Patch
Fading-out	Yellowed areas in grass	Fungus—thrives in hot, humid weather	Use Captan, PMA or treat same as brown patch
Leaf Spot	Dark red or purple spots on leaves and stems, prevalent in Kentucky bluegrass	Fungus—at its worst in cool, wet weather	Mow at 2 inches, treat same as fading out, Merion blue is resistant
Rust	Orange or brown powdery markings on leaves and stems, prevalent in Merion bluegrass	Fungus—thrives late in summer when dew is heavy	Use Zineb, Kentucky blue is more resistant
Pythium Blight	Greasy looking spots and patches on water soaked leaves	Fungus—most destructive in warm, wet weather	If Dexon or Zineb do not alleviate, lawn will need renovation

Lawn Diseases and Their Control *(Continued)*

Disease	Damage	Cause	Control
Snow Mold Fusarium Patch	White growth on leaves turn to light brown and leaves cling together	Fungus—thrives when green grass is covered by snow	Same as Brown Patch

LAWN PESTS AND THEIR CONTROL

Pest	Damage	Description	Control
Chinch Bugs	Small yellow patches that turn to brown dead areas	Tiny pink, red or brown bugs with white branded backs	Chlordane, Sevin or Dieldrin
Grubs	Large brown irregular-shaped patches	Whitish with brown heads. Lie curled in "C" position	Heptachlor, Aldrin Chlordane or Dieldrin
Sod Webworms	Small brown spots with irregular grass growth	Light brown larvae about ¾" long become caterpillars	Same as Grubs
Cutworms	Similar to sod webworms	Brown, grey or black ½" long caterpillars	Same as Sod Webworms
Ants	Dirt mounds, grass root destruction	Various familiar species	Same as Grubs
Wireworms	Withered and dying grass from boring into roots	Dark brown, slender larvae 1½" long	Same as Sod Webworms
Armyworms	Round bare spots in lawn	Green with black striped larvae 1½" long	Same as Sod Webworms

SHRUB AND TREE PESTS AND THEIR CONTROL

Pest	Plants Affected	Damage	Description	Control
Aphids	Almost all shrubs and trees	Sucks juices from plants and steals vigor, leaves and buds become disfigured, carries other diseases	Tiny, green lice-like with wings	Use Rotenone, Lindane, Malathion or Pyrethrum
Bagworms	Arborvitae, hemlock, juniper, pine, spruce, locust, linden, maple, sycamore	Eats foliage, can quickly defoliate good-sized tree	Brown caterpillar, in cocoon-bag one inch	Use Malathion or Lead Arsenate. Handpick and destroy bags
Tent Caterpillar	Apple, birch, elm, oak, pear, plum, hawthorn, flowering crab, cherry	Eats foliage, can defoliate large tree in very short time	Black caterpillars with white stripe down back—yellow brown on side	Remove and burn tents and caterpillars. use DDT or Lead Arsenate
Cankerworms (Fall and Spring) (Inchworms)	Apple, elm, oak, birch, linden, maple, cherry, plum, beech, hawthorn	Eats foliage, can defoliate large trees, droppings are black pellets	Green with yellow stripe drop from branches on silken thread	Use DDT or Lead Arsenate
Webworms	Most deciduous shrubs and trees	Skeletonizes leaves, ties leaves with webs	Hairy greenish worms with black stripes and spots	Use DDT, Methoxychlor or Sevin
Spider Mites		(see Roses)		
Lace Bugs	Andromeda, azalea, oak, sycamore, elm, hawthorn, rhododendron, cotoneaster, mountain laurel, linden	Sucks juices from underside of leaves, leaves turn yellow with gummy residue on undersides	Tiny insects with lace-like look in wings	Use Malathion, Sevin or Lindane

Shrub and Tree Pests and Their Control (*Continued*)

Pest	Plants Affected	Damage	Description	Control
Japanese Beetle	Elm, flowering crab, horse chestnut, willow, apple, grape, current, peach	(see Roses)		
Thrips	Privet and other shrubs	(see Roses)		
Borers	Rhododendron, dogwood, lilac, sycamore, maple, ash, oak, willow, peach, apricot	Tunnel under bark, eat into living tree tissue, ridges appear under bark, leaves curl and brown	Tiny with minute wings	Avoid bark injury, spray trunk with DDT, cut out infested areas and paint with tree wound paint

SHRUB AND TREE DISEASES AND THEIR CONTROL

Disease	Plants Affected	Damage	Cause	Control
Wilt	Azalea, barberry, maple, oak	Yellowing of leaves, stunted plants. Leaves drop first on one side then on other	Fungus, lives in soil, enters roots	Grow resistant varieties, plant only in clean soil or fumigate soil, spraying does little good
Leaf Spot	Mock orange, rhododendron, laurel, leucothoe, hydrangea, boxwood, viburnum, azalea, holly, camelia, elm, dogwood	Small round spots with light tan centers. Brown borders on leaves	Fungus	Use Zineb or Ferbam

217

Shrub and Tree Diseases and Their Control (*Continued*)

Disease	Plants Affected	Damage	Cause	Control
Bacterial Leaf Spot	Barberry, viburnum	Small irregular spots on leaves. Goes from green to brown	Bacteria	Use Bordeaux mixture
Fireblight	Cotoneaster, firethorn, crabapple, pear, hawthorn, mountain ash, apple	Leaves wilt as if scorched by fire. Leaves do not fall	Bacteria	Spray with Streptomycin solution
Blossom and Twig Blight	Flowering almond	Powdery brown spores. Twigs and leaves brown and die	Fungus	Use Captan just before blossoms open
Powdery Mildew	Apple, azalea, crapemyrtle, euonymous, grapes, honeysuckle, hydrangea, lilac, rhododendron, viburnum, holly, sycamore	Patches of white powder on leaves, dwarfs and disfigures plants	Fungus, thrives in cool, wet weather and shady areas	Use Karathane or wettable Sulfur regularly
Chlorosis	Azalea, camellia, gardenia, magnolia, hydrangea, oak, rhododendron	Leaves become yellow, often appears on plants grown close to house foundations	Too high alkaline content in soil	Use Iron Chelates on plant and surrounding soil
Dieback	Boxwood, rhododendron	Branches change color, becoming tan and die	Various funguses	Remove all dead material and burn, use Bordeaux mixture
Bud and Twig Blight	Azalea, privet, juniper	Ends of buds and twigs turn brown, fungus continues to grow into twig and can kill plant	Fungus, spread by moisture	Remove infected material and burn

ROSE PESTS AND THEIR CONTROL

Pest	Damage	Description	Control
Aphids	Sucks juices from plants and cause leaves and buds to become disfigured, carries other diseases	Tiny, green lice-like bugs with wings	Use Rotenone, Lindane, Malathion or Pyrethrum
Rose Chafer	Eats flowers, and leaves, can completely defoliate plant	Grey, long-legged beetle, ½ inch	Use DDT or Methoxychlor
Japanese Beetle	Eats flowers and leaves, often completely	Metalic green with conspicuous white spots, 1 inch	Hand pick if possible, use DDT or Methoxychlor
Rose Curculio	Eats holes in buds and leaves, buds never open	Red, snouted beetles with black legs, ¼ inch	Use DDT
Rose Leafhopper	Sucks juices from underside of leaves, turn faded, then yellow, brown and die	Greenish, wedge shaped, ⅛ inch	Use DDT, Pyrethrum, Methoxychlor or Rotenone
Rose Scale	Sucks plant juices, weaken and can kill plant	White, round scaly insect, ⅛ inch across	Remove and burn infested areas, dormant spray in spring, later use Malathion
Rose Slug	Skeletonizes leaves and eat large holes in edge of leaf	Yellow-green, many species, about ½ to 1 inch	Use Malathion, or Arsenate of lead
Thrips	Feeds only on flowers, buds turn brown and fail to open	Tiny yellow orange	Cut off diseased buds, use Lindane or Malathion
Rose Midge	Eats buds which then turn black, bloom stops	Tiny yellow brown	Use DDT

Rose Pests and Their Control *(Continued)*

Pest	Damage	Description	Control
Spider Mites	Feeds on underside of leaves, leaves become grey, red or brown, can defoliate entire plant	Very tiny (almost invisible to naked eye) oval	Use Malathion, Kelthane or DDT
Rose Stem Girdler	Tunnels into stem, shoots swell up	Small white caterpillars	Cut off and burn all infected shoots

ROSE DISEASES AND THEIR CONTROL

Disease	Damage	Cause	Control
Black Spot	Black spots on leaves, leaves turn yellow and fall	Fungus, thrives in cool, wet weather	Rake leaves and burn, use Captan or Fermate
Anthracnose	Dark spots with light centers on leaves and canes	Fungus, thrives in cool, wet weather	Same as Black Spot
Brown Canker	White spots with purple outside ring on canes and leaves, can kill plant	Fungus	Remove all diseased canes, use Bordeaux mixture, use no mulch
Stem Canker	Purple stripe on branches, become brown and girdles plant	Fungus	Cut off entire area to point below infection, use Captan
Mildew	White powdery areas turn black, dwarfs leaves, disfigures buds	Fungus, thrives in cool, wet weather	Use Karathane or Piprin as soon as noticed, use Captan later
Rust	Orange spots on leaves and canes, can kill plant	Fungus, thrives in cool, wet weather	Remove and burn leaves, use Zineb or Bordeaux mixture
Leaf Spot	Brown spots with gray centers, leaves turn brown and fall	Fungus, carried on seed and remains in soil	Remove and burn diseased leaves, use Maneb or Zineb

FLOWER PESTS AND THEIR CONTROL

Pest	Plants Affected	Damage	Description	Control
Aphids	Almost all flowers	Sucks juices from plants and causes leaves and buds to become disfigued, carries other diseases	(see Roses)	
Blister Beetles	Aster, calendula, marigold, phlox, zinnia	Eats leaves	(see Beets)	
Stalk Borers	Aster, columbine, cosmos, dahlia, delphinium, iris; hollyhock, zinnia	Bores into stalks and can kill plant, makes small hole in stalk and leaves droppings around hole.	Brown caterpillar with brown or purple stripes 1 inch	Keep area very clean and weed free, use DDT or Sevin
Cutworms	Affects many plants including aster, carnation, dahlia, zinnia	Cuts off plants at ground level, can destroy several plants each night	Brown, or gray smooth worms with sucker-like apparatus on underside, 1 to 2 inches	Put Chlordane or Dieldrin around base of plants when setting out
Leafhoppers	Asters, calendula, dahlia, gladiolus, marigold, zinnia	Leaves curl and turn yellow, plants may die	(see Beans)	
Japanese Beetles	Many plants	Eats flowers and leaves, often completely	(see Roses)	
Leafminers	Aster, columbine, gladiolus, snapdragon, also common on birch and other trees	Feeds on leaves and are seen as trails in top side of leaves	Tiny white maggots	Use Malathion as soon as tunnels appear, systemics especially good here

Flower Pests and Their Control (*Continued*)

Pest	Plants Affected	Damage	Description	Control
Thrips	Ageratum, alyssum, aster, bulbs, chrysanthemums, dahlia, dianthus, gladiolus, marigold	Feeds on flowers, buds turn brown and fail to open	(see Roses)	
Spider Mites	Almost all plants	Feeds on underside of leaves which become grey, red or brown, can defoliate an entire plant	(see Roses)	

FLOWER DISEASES AND THEIR CONTROL

Disease	Plants Affected	Damage	Cause	Control
Leaf Spot	Aster, calendula, chrysanthemum, cosmos, dahlia, daisy, delphinium, dianthus, geranium, gladiolus, hollyhock, iris, marigold, pansy, phlox, poppy, zinnia	Small round spots with light tan centers, brown borders on leaves	(see Roses)	
Powdery Mildew	Alyssum, calendula, chrysanthemum, cosmos, dahlia, daisy, delphinium, phlox, poppy, snapdragon, sweet pea, zinnia	Patches of white powder on leaves, dwarfs and disfigures plants	(see Shrubs and Trees)	

Flower Diseases and Their Control (*Continued*)

Disease	Damage	Plants Affected	Cause	Control
Rust	Orange or brown powdery markings on leaves and stems	Alyssum, aster, chrysanthemum, dianthus, hollyhock, snapdragon	(see Roses)	
Wilt	Yellowing of leaves, stunted plants, leaves start to drop on one side then on the other	Alyssum, aster, chrysanthemum, columbine, dahlia, dianthus, marigold, peony, snapdragon	(see Shrubs and Trees)	
Virus Diseases	Yellows foliage, mottles leaves distorts plant parts	Virtually all plants affected to one degree or another	Various viruses	Use resistant plants only, keep planting areas clean and weed free, burn diseased plants
Blights	Spotting and wilting—usually sudden— of foliage, flowers, stems	Chrysanthemum, dahlia, gladiolus, peony, snapdragon	Fungus, thrives in high humidity, low air circulation areas	Use Captan or Zineb
Bulb Rot	Bulbs, corms and tubers rot and may have an offensive odor	Many flowers grown from bulbs, etc.	Bacteria or later stage of other disease	Destroy bulbs or corms affected, some tubers and rhizomes can be treated with Captan, Ferbam or Zineb
Nematodes	Yellowing, loss of vigor, and wilting in hot weather	Most plants can be affected	Tiny worm-like plant parasites found in most soils	Use resistant varieties, check for type of nematode or soil fumigant with county agent

VEGETABLE DISEASES AND THEIR CONTROL

Disease	Damage	Plant Affected	Cause	Control
Rust	Orange or brown powdery markings on leaves and stems	Asparagus, beans	Fungus, thrives in moist weather	Grow rust resistant varieties, use Bordeaux mixture or Sulfur solution
Wilt	Yellowing leaves, stunted plants, lower leaves start to drop	Cabbage, eggplant, potato, corn, tomato, watermelon	Fungus, lives in soil, enters roots	Grow resistant varieties, plant seed in clean soil or fumigate soil, spraying does little good
Mosaic	Mottled, curled leaves, stunted plants, reduced yields	Cucumbers, beans, peas, tomatoes, potatoes, peppers, squash, melon	Virus, spread by plant lice (Aphids)	Spray regularly with Malathion or Lindane —follow directions carefully
Leaf Spot	Small round spots with light tan centers, brown borders on leaves	Beets, melon, peppers, tomatoes	Fungus	Use Bordeaux mixture or fixed copper fungicide
Anthracnose	Brown sunken spots with pink centers	Bean, pepper, watermelon, cucumber	Fungus, thrives in cool, wet weather	Do not work in garden when plants are wet-spreads disease, use Zineb
Blight	Dark irregular dead areas on leaves and stem	Celery, tomatoes, potatoes	Fungus, thrives in cool, wet weather	Use Bordeaux mixture or fixed copper fungicide, grow resistant varieties

VEGETABLE PESTS AND THEIR CONTROL

Plant Affected	Damage	Pest & Description	Control
Asparagus	Holes eaten in foliage	Asparagus beetle, blue-black bug ¼ inch with yellow markings	Use Rotenone, DDT or Malathion
Beans	Leaves skeletonized, pods and underside of leaves eaten	Mexican bean beetle, black spots on deep orange colored bug, ¼ inch	Use Rotenone, Malathion or Sevin
	Regular-shaped holes eaten in leaves	Bean leaf beetle, black spots on reddish bug, ¼ inch	Use Sevin, DDT or Malathion
	Leaves curl and turn yellow, plants may die	Leafhoppers, green, wedge-shaped ⅛ inch	Use Sevin, DDT or Malathion
	Bores into seed and stops development	Seed corn maggot, yellow, no legs ¼ inch	Treat seed with Dieldrin before planting, wait for warm weather before planting
	Leaves curl and turn yellow, can spread mosaic	Bean aphid, tiny black insect, clusters on leaves	Use Malathion
Beets	Eats leaves and buds, ties folded leaves with web	Beet webworm, greenish with black stripe and spots 1¼ inches	Use Pyrethrum
	Eats leaves	Blister beetles, gray striped ¾ inch	Use Methoxychlor
Broccoli	(see Cabbage)		
Brussels Sprouts	(see Cabbage)		
Cabbage	Curled leaves turn yellow, stunts plant	Cabbage aphid, tiny green insect-clusters on leaves	Use Malathion
	Eats ragged holes, bores into head	Cabbage looper, green worm loops to crawl, 1½ inches	Use Malathion or Methoxychlor

Vegetable Pests and Their Control *(Continued)*

Plant Affected	Damage	Pest & Description	Control
Cabbage	Same as Looper	Cabbageworm, green worm, 1½ inches	Same as Looper
	Plants wilt, leaves turn brown	Harlequin bug, black with red or yellow, ⅜ inch	Handpick bugs and use Naled
	Bores into buds and stems, kills plants	Cabbage webworm, yellow with purple stripes, ½ inch	Use DDT, Malathion or Methoxychlor
	Causes roots to rot, plants wilt and die	Root maggots, white, no legs, ¼ inch	Treat soil with Chlordane when sprouts appear
	Eats leaves, makes trail of slime	Slugs, gray slimy, legless bodies	Use bait containing Metaldehyde
Cantaloupe	(see Cucumber)		
Carrots	Digs into fleshy roots	Carrot rust fly, yellow, no legs ⅓ inch	Place Diazinon in seed furrows at planting time
	Destroys tops	Carrot caterpillar, green with black and yellow stripes, 2 inches	Handpick
	Spreads yellow virus	Leafhoppers, greenish wedge shaped black spots, ⅛ inch	Use Sevin or DDT
Cauliflower	(see Cabbage)		
Celery	Eats holes in leaves and stalks, rolls leaves and ties with web	Leaf tier, green wormlike, ¾ inch	Use Pyrethrum or DDT
Corn	Feeds on shoots, later eats corn kernels near tip	Corn earworm, brown or pink worm with light stripes, 2 inches	Early season use DDT, use Sevin as soon as silks appear
	Eats stalks and kernels	Corn borer, pink or brown with brownhead, 1 inch	Use DDT spray regularly

Vegetable Pests and Their Control *(Continued)*

Plant Affected	Damage	Pest & Description	Control
	Bores into seed and stops development	Seed corn maggot, yellow no legs, ¼ inch	Treat seed with Dieldrin before planting, wait for warm weather for planting
Cucumbers	Eats leaves, stems, fruit, plants wilt and die	Striped cucumber beetle, yellow with 3 black stripes, ¼ inch	Use Sevin, Malathion or Methoxychlor
	Tunnels into all parts of plant	Pickleworm, white with brown head, ¾ inch	Use Sevin or Malathion
Eggplant	(see Tomatoes)		
Lettuce		Cabbage looper (see Cabbage)	Use Malathion or Methoxychlor
		Leafhopper (see Carrots)	Use Sevin or DDT
Onions	Sucks juice from plant causes white blotches then withering	Thrips, tiny, yellow with wings	Use DDT or Malathion
Peas	Eats blossoms and burrows into seed	Weevil, brown with markings ¼ inch	Use DDT, Malathion or Methoxychlor
Peppers	(see Tomatoes)		
Potatoes	Eats all leaves	Potato beetle, yellow with black stripe, ½ inch	Handpick if possible, use Sevin or DDT
		Blister beetles (see Beets)	Use Methoxy-chlor
		Leaf hoppers (see Beans)	Use Sevin or DDT
Pumpkins		(see Cucumbers)	

Vegetable Pests and Their Control *(Continued)*

Plant Affected	Damage	Pest & Description	Control
Radish	Tunnels into roots	Maggots, yellow, no legs ¼ inch	Use Chlordane as directed
Rhubarb	Punctures into stems	Curculio, beetle with snout, powdery yellow, ¾ inch	Hand pick
Spinach		(see Beets)	
Squash (see Cucumbers)	Sucks sap from leaves and stems, plants wilt and die	Squash bug, brown with flat back ¾ inch	Hand pick, use Sevin or Malathion
Tomatoes		Fruitworm, same as corn earworm	Use DDT or Savin
		Potato beetle (see Potatoes)	Handpick or use DDT or Sevin
	Eats tunnel into stem, plant withers and dies	Stalk borer, white with purple back, 1¼ inches	Use DDT
	Eats foliage and fruit	Hornworms, green with long horn on rear end	Hand pick, use DDT
		Blister beetles (see Beets)	Use Methoxychlor
	Eats small holes	Flea beetles, small, many species	Use DDT
Watermelon		(see Cucumbers)	

CHAPTER 11

Garden Calendar

Gardening is many things to many people, and can, therefore, be exactly what you want it to be. It is your decision to make; a year round, every spare moment occupation, a once-in-a-while hobby, a weekends only type of thing, or a whenever-you-get-caught task. Whichever classification best suits your tastes, time and talents, certain gardening activities should be accomplished at specific times of the year. That is, if you want to be able to brag about the results.

The gardening calendar presented here is designed specifically for the new homeowner and beginning gardener. It tells him, in capsule form how to do the right things at the right time, not matter the scope of his ambitions. It is, however, only a stepping stone, for as the greenhorn develops into a back-fence expert, and then into a gardener, experience along with trials, errors and tribulations will add many entries to this list.

Because each part of the country has widely varying temperatures and environmental conditions, the calendar suggestions should be tempered with common sense and frequent checks of the thermometer. Starting too early can be considerably more harmful than starting a bit late. As anxious and enthused as you may be, don't start too soon—you will have all summer to regret your haste.

JANUARY

Not much can be accomplished outdoors during this month, but this can be made up in indoor activity. Plans for the coming season should be started, and all basic preparations gotten under way. Send for and thoroughly examine seed-company and nursery catalogs. Select the seed and plants that best fit your plan. Order correct amounts using the guides presented in the catalogs, select the varieties suggested as best for your location, and buy only from reliable sources. If you plan to start vegetable or flower seed indoors for later transplanting, be certain the necessary equipment and materials are on hand when you want them—peat pots, soil, vermiculite, sand, clear plastic bags and sheets, and of course, the seed.

Try to make a quick tour of your property after each heavy snowfall. Be especially alert to snow piled on evergreens and foundation plantings. Brush heavy snow from branches and limbs to prevent breakage. Replace any mulching materials that may have been moved by wind or rain. Check to see that bushes and shrubs have not been heaved by alternate thawing and freezing. Tamp any heaved plants back into position.

If shrubs and trees were not protected earlier, do it now, if at all possible. Tree wrap paper on young tree trunks will prevent sunscald and cracking; burlap or plastic spray (apply only when temperature is over 40°) will keep trees and shrubs from drying out; mulching will keep the ground temperature relatively even, preventing heaving; and bracing and guying will keep trees from damage caused by violent windstorms and accumulations of snow.

Take special notice and care of house plants. Water often, but do not overwater. Plants require more frequent watering because of the warm, dry air prevalent in most modern homes. Keep the soil moist, but not so moist that it becomes waterlogged.

In warm climates, dormant spraying can be done, some very hardy vegetables planted, and trees, shrubs, and bushes pruned and cleaned out.

FEBRUARY

Still not too much that can be done outdoors, but continue a program of preventive maintenance. If you planted spring flowering bulbs in the fall, check their location to be certain they have not started to grow causing them to break ground prematurely. If they have started to show through the soil, and freezing weather is still to come, cover the entire planted area with a three-inch layer of mulch, either peat moss, hay, or whatever else is available.

This is a good month to make sure all tools and equipment are in shape and ready for action. That is, not only gardening hardware, but also outdoor furniture, swings, sandpiles or boxes, etc. Inspect everything that is to be used outdoors, and either repair or replace any items not in first-class condition. All power equipment should be rechecked, and if any doubt exists concerning top operation, send for a reliable repairman.

In warm climates, dormant spraying should be completed if it has not already been done, and pruning of trees and shrubs begun. All but the very tender vegetable seeds should be sown late in the month, and general cleanup of outdoor areas (lawn, gardens, patios, play area) completed. If the ground is not too wet, this is a good time to start a lawn renovation program.

MARCH

Nice, warm days will soon start you itching to work outdoors. The day-dreaming and planning should be done by now, and the work, in earnest, should begin. However, don't be tricked into a headlong "de-winterization" of your trees, shrubs, flowers, etc. Winter protection in the form of coverings, mulches, and wind barriers should not be re-moved all at once,—remove gradually, as an insurance measure against an unexpected killing cold snap.

Spray trees, shrubs and bushes with a dormant oil spray mixture. Thoroughly cover all sides of limbs and branches with the oil spray. Check the weather forecast prior to spraying, and do not spray if temperature will fall below 40° within 24 hours. The spray will control scale diseases on trees and shrubs and kill many wintering-over insects.

Clean up the lawn by raking briskly, or give lawn area a quick once over with a power rake or thatcher. Any bare lawn spots, or lawn areas winter-killed should be spot renovated at this time. Break up the soil in dead lawn areas, turn over, fertilize, lime, smooth out, broadcast seed, tamp down, water, and hope for grass. The remainder of the lawn should be fertilized late in March, and if a soil test indicates the requirements, add lime.

Most pruning of trees and shrubs is done at this time, just before new growth begins. Pruning should be done carefully, accurately, and accord-ing to recognized techniques. Too much or too little pruning can ruin an otherwise healthy plant. Protect all pruned cuts over pencil thickness with tree-wound paint or similar preparation.

As soon as the soil dries out enough to permit working, planting can begin. Plant roses, trees, shrubs, and any of the hardier vegetables and flowers. Check tulip and other bulb beds and remove heavy mulching materials after the first few bulb shoots break the surface.

In the South, work should be well under way planting vegetable gardens, fertilizing lawns and trees, and setting out annual and peren-nial plants. A regular spraying program should be instituted at this time and continued religiously for the remainder of the growing season. All warm-weather plants, trees, and shrubs should be planted and thoroughly watered down. Just about everything should be in full swing or rapidly moving forward if garden plans stand any chance of completion.

APRIL

For April showers to bring May flowers, be very sure to get your seed planting done in April. In addition, roses, trees, shrubs, bushes, annuals and perennials should be planted and carefully tended this month. Hold off until the end of the month to plant the very tender varieties. Continue to sow vegetables outside, but here too, the tender ones including melons, tomatoes, cucumbers, beans, etc., should be held until all danger of frost is past.

By the end of the month, no trees, shrubs, or roses that have been packed and sold bare-root should be planted, since the chance of success is greatly reduced. If you have been unable to get your plants into the ground by this time, plant only those that have been balled and burlapped or containerized.

A word of caution: Do not overdo the heavy work in those first few days outdoors. Charley horses, stiff backs, and a peculiar gait called the "Homeowner's Shuffle" are the result of doing too much too soon after a long winter of relative idleness. A bit better planning of your time schedule and heeding your wife's "I think that's enough for today, dear" will stand you in good stead.

The spraying program should continue and should now include fruit trees, ornamentals, roses, and flowering shrubs. Add a fungicide, such as fermate, to the insecticide spray to insure that mildew does not take its toll.

If not already done, lawn maintenance and renovation should be completed early this month. Pre-emergence crabgrass killers should be put down, and other lawn chores completed. If you plan to use one of the combination fertilizer-crabgrass killers, the sooner you get this onto the lawn, the greater the chance for success. If at all possible, do not mow the lawn so grass growth can get a good headstart, and water consistently and thoroughly.

In the South and other warm areas, move rapidly toward the end of all planting: finish planting gladiolus at two weeks intervals (so they don't all bloom at the same time and then—nothing), plant annuals (tender and hardy plants), and all remaining vegetable seeds and seedlings. Keep close tabs on your spraying program and be sure to spray at least once each week and after every heavy rainfall. (This is a good job for your wife to tackle. The new lightweight sprayers are easy to handle and carry, and the whole job can be accomplished with a minimum of fuss and effort, saving valuable weekend time for other jobs). Dusing of vegetables should start, this being done during the late afternoon on days with little or no wind. Again, timing makes this a very good job for wife or older child.

If not already started, apply generous amounts of mulch around roses, trees, most vegetables and other plantings. Any of various locally available mulches will do a good job, and those such as pine bark mulch will keep down weeds, maintain soil temperatures, help the soil retain moisture, and enhance the physical looks of most garden areas.

MAY

For best results this season, and indeed, this year, this is just about your last chance for planting. Toward the end of May very warm weather starts, so it is best to forget all planting until the fall when cooler, wetter weather arrives. If you must plant late in May, be certain to water the plants well after planting, and continue to water on a regular basis.

Gladiolus corms can be planted throughout June for successive blooms, but you should complete all other planting as quickly as possible. Set tender annuals and vegetables directly into the ground, and transfer bedding plants to their permanent summer locations.

This is the season of magnificent spring flowering bulbs, so if you planted bulbs last fall, enjoy the fruits of your labor. After blooming, tulips should be checked carefully and all seed heads removed so plant strength will not be sapped by seed making. If tulips must be moved from a flower bed to make room, remove carefully, leaving soil around the roots, and replant in a group, in a well watered, shady spot until leaves are brown. Then dig up, clean, and store for fall planting. Do not remove the leaves of any of the spring flowering bulbs after they have flowered; the green leaves make food required for the next year's blooms. Wait until all leaves are brown and withered before cleaning them out of the garden.

Maintain your scheduled spraying program. To benefit most plants, add a soluble fertilizer to the insecticide, fungicide or miticide spray, and take care of two jobs at one time. Check large shade trees to be certain there will be no trouble with insects, and dust or spray vegetable gardens.

Thin out vegetable and flower seedlings to recommended spacing. Remove flowers from newly planted strawberry plants and give yourself a better chance of large, sweet berries later in the year. Watch newly planted tomato plants carefully and protect with hotcaps or plastic bags if very cold nights are forecast. Keep vegetable gardens clean and as weed free as possible. Grass clippings from clean lawns make good mulch, and will help keep weeds to a minimum in a vegetable garden.

One of the typical "Saturday morning in the suburbs" sounds is the noisy buzz of lawn mowers chomping away. Lawn mowing time is here. Do not cut the grass, especially new grass, any closer than about 2 inches. Maintain this grass height throughout the summer, but if drought conditions continue, raise the blade height a bit to help insure that grass is not killed by lack of water.

Warmer areas of the country should be well into the growing season by now. Spraying, fertilizing and watering are musts and should be accomplished on a planned basis. Weeding can become an almost full time job now, so mulch and spray where possible to keep down or eliminate many weeds. For best results with roses, debud often. The remaining buds will produce blooms of a truly prize-winning size.

JUNE

This is the month of garden action. All danger of frost is past, so everything should be in the ground and prospering mightily. Some fertilizer and considerable watering should keep flowers, vegetables, trees and shrubs moving right along. Continue a spraying program so your efforts are not negated by bugs, pests, or diseases.

By this time, the leaves of spring-flowering bulbs should be brown, indicating it is time to remove and store those that will not winter over. Up to now, the bulb, through the green leaves, has been manufacturing and storing food for the next season's growth. Once brown and withered, dig them up, clean them thoroughly and store in a cool dry place. Wintering over bulbs should have their withered leaves removed, but otherwise should be left alone unless transplanting to another location is desired.

Speaking of bulbs, this month is a fine time to plant the tender, summer flowering bulbs such as caladiums and begonias. Plant at the correct depth for each specific bulb type, add some bone meal to well mixed soil, and water well.

June is also the rose month, so, in return for a reasonable amount of work, expect the maximum of color, beauty and enjoyment from your roses. If you have not mulched around your rose bushes, wait no longer, do it immediately. Use any of the many mulching materials available, but whatever you select, get it down, and water well. Weed thoroughly before mulching and all you should have to worry about after this is an occasional weed that has not gotten the mulch message. The weed and feed chemicals currently available do a good "double-duty" job, especially in and around rose gardens.

Keep your rose bushes well watered, well sprayed, and well tended for the ultimate in number and quality of blooms. Remove all faded blossoms as quickly as possible. Cut roses so at least two five part leaves remain under the point of the cut. Continue to spray for insects, diseases and fungus problems by using either a combination spray or separate applications of specific chemicals.

Spend extra time now in cleaning, trimming and maintaining your property. Shrubs that have become scraggly should be clipped. Be sure to cut the top a bit narrower than the bottom so sunlight can get at all parts of the shrub. Clean out flower beds periodically so no spent blooms are around to spoil the overall appearance. Apply mulches where required, and keep an eye out for those previously mulched areas which may need filling in.

In the warmer parts of the country, this is the time for watering, fertilizing, and general care and maintenance. By this time gardeners should be able to estimate the degree of success they can expect from their gardens, but they can still make or break these plantings with actions this month. Watering should be regular, heavy, and deep. Fertilize now, but check each plant's requirements to be certain the time is right.

Spraying should continue so you remain even in the war against insects, pests and diseases. Select and pick many vegetables and flowers with the happy thought that there are even better days ahead.

JULY

Considerable time and effort should be spent this month in caring for and maintaining the plants that are now coming into their full glory. Whatever else is on your gardening schedule, do not neglect to water thoroughly and often during this hot, dry month. The obvious places, such as lawns, gardens, and flowers beds should be given as much water as possible. However, do not forget the less obvious places, for trees, evergreens, shrubs and other plantings require considerable amounts of water during these dry periods. For the greatest benefit to evergreens, trees, shrubs, etc., water deeply so the water gets to the roots. The best way to do this is also the most obvious—use a root feeder. This is a tool that is pushed into the ground, all around the tree you wish to water, getting the water where it will do the most good.

In areas affected by water restrictions, mulching can often mean the difference between life and death to your plants. By maintaining whatever little water is available, mulches play vital roles during droughts. Whichever one of the many available mulches you select, lay it down thick, at least two inches, and preferably just after a rain or a soaking so the maximum amount of water can be maintained in the soil.

Keep after your lawn this month—water well and weed carefully, but do not fertilize. Fertilizing this month will ensure some prize winning weeds, but little else of value. During the hottest parts of the month, mowing need not be as often, but should not be neglected. An extra day or two between mowings will do considerably more good than harm. Similarly, do not cut the grass as short as normally, but instead raise the mower blade one-half to one inch for use throughout this month.

In the warmer parts of the country gardeners should content themselves with the bounty of their labors and maintain a strict schedule of watering, weeding and spraying. This is also a good time to sit back a bit, relax, and browse through a bulb catalog. It is not too early for the southern gardener to select and order fall-planted, spring-flowering bulbs. Most of the labor and costs are behind you and seeing the results should raise your enthusiasm so you can't wait for the next growing season.

AUGUST

Maintenance, watering, fertilizing and spraying should continue throughout this month, and if you can continue your schedule conscientiously, the odds are in your favor for a successful gardening season. Now there is time left for just looking and enjoying, so make the most of this pleasure time while it lasts.

Late in the month is a good time to plant evergreens. This will give the transplants time to get settled and get a good hold in their new environment before cold weather comes and virtually stops everything. Plant the evergreens deep, but not too deeply. A good rule of thumb is to plant the evergreens just a bit deeper than the soil mark indicates they were at the nursery. After planting, water well and daily, if possible, and ring them with heavy layers of mulching material.

This is also a good time to take cuttings to make house plants for indoor greenery all year long. In most locations these plants will get a bare minimum of sunlight indoors, so supplement, if possible, with Gro-Lux bulbs. Incidentally, as these plants grow, you can keep taking more and more cuttings so when spring arrives, you will have increased the number of beautiful coleus, ageratum, waxed begonias or whatever, for setting outdoors in your flower beds. And, you can't beat the price.

Late August is another of the preparation months. If seeding or re-seeding is required on your lawn, start the process in late August by grading, smoothing, liming, fertilizing and anything else necessary as preparation for the seeding. Then, late in September you are ready to complete the job with seeding, light raking and watering.

Watch rose bushes carefully this month, for humid, sticky weather is a fine incubator for blackspot. Continued spraying and watering—only at ground level, not on the foliage—should prevent the start of this infection and keep your bushes healthy for their spectacular September show.

In the country's warmer areas the whole list of fall vegetables should be seeded. Sow seeds of cucumbers, many beans, turnips, cabbage and many others. Put in plants rather than seed for vegetables like tomatoes and collards, since they take a bit longer to develop.

SEPTEMBER

This is a busy month for the gardener, for much of next year's results will depend upon the work and preparation completed now. The onset of cool weather marks the arrival of diverse garden activities: lawn rejuvenation time, rose, evergreen and tree planting time, and harvest time for many fruits and vegetables.

September weather, the beautiful early fall kind that makes you glad you own a piece of land (no matter how small), is the best time of the year to put in a new lawn or repair or rejuvenate an old one. Remember though, that merely spreading some seed will do you no good. For new lawns, follow carefully the suggestions in Chapter 4. For established lawns, a thorough going over with a thatcher, followed by cleaning and fertilizing, seeding and watering should get good results. Whatever your situation—new or established lawn—do a thorough job. Lick and promise efforts result in little but wasted time, energy and money.

All new plantings, be they roses, shrubs or trees should be watered deeply and often. It is not wise to apply mulch at this time, either to new transplants or established plants. The addition of mulch will lengthen the amount of time necessary for the plants to harden off, making the plant susceptible to damage from the first heavy frost. All mulch, therefore, should be withheld until after the plant wood has had enough time to harden off. When the ground is frozen, a layer of mulch is applied.

Now is the time for some bulbs to come out and others to go in. Tuberous begonias, gladioli and all other tender bulbs are removed from the ground after the foliage has wilted or been touched by frost. Clean the bulbs thoroughly, dust with DDT and put them into a clean dry place in string bags. Spring flowering bulbs and other hardy species are planted now with a bit of bonemeal, mulched over and left alone until spring.

Keep after your roses. They will continue blooming beautifully, but watering and spraying must continue unabated. Chrysanthemums too should be coming into their own, so if you have planted them in out of the way places, and want some fall color, dig them with a large root ball, replant immediately, and water well.

It is a wise idea to keep close tabs on the weather predictions at this time of year, especially those of nighttime temperatures. If the temperature is scheduled to drop very low and your vegetables (like tomatoes) and some pretty flowers are worth saving, cover with paper hats, bushel baskets or other protection. If done quickly and efficiently just prior to frost, many plants and vegetables can be saved.

In the South, saving is also the order of the day, especially where tulips and some other bulbs are concerned. For best results, or more accurately for any results at all, put new tulip bulbs in cold storage until late December, and plant then. If you do not do this, the chances of success with the bulbs is slight. However, it is neither too early nor too late to continue planting gladiolus, nor for that matter most of the other spring flowering bulbs: Iris, crocus, hyacinth, narcissus, and ranunculus.

Continue with garden chores—watering and spraying since the long season requires longer periods of prescribed garden work.

OCTOBER

All the productive work should be done by now, and because the colder weather permits steadily decreasing periods of work in the garden, make the most of the time to thoroughly clean-up the garden and other areas around the outside of the house. If you are making a compost heap for eventual addition of humus to the garden soil, most of your garden vegetative debris can be heaped on the pile. If not, it should be collected and carefully burned. While you are out in the garden turn over the soil, leaving the soil in large clods. The alternate freezing and thawing aids the soil and at the same time rids it of unwanted insects and bugs.

Mound up rose bushes with soil put aside for that purpose, just after the ground freezes. Do not cut back rose canes at this time, but keep full height until spring. By doing this, winter kill on roses occurs at tops of canes and not lower down.

Fertilize trees late in the month, but make sure it is done late enough not to encourage new growth that will be killed off by frost. Very late feeding will allow trees to store food and develop strong roots without causing damage to trees through killing off of new growth.

Keep lawns free of matted grass and fallen leaves. Heavy matted grass or wet leaves can smother grass, especially tender new grass, so be sure to keep lawns clean and debris free.

Check out all garden tools and equipment and start to winterize. Drain gasoline from mower, clean and put away for next year. Thoroughly clean all other tools and wipe them with a protective layer of oil or grease and store in a dry place.

Southern gardeners are now enjoying roses and other blooms, so watering continues to be important. Fertilizing should be avoided. Spring-flowering bulbs should be planted now, and other bulbs lifted, cleaned and stored for next year. Anything planted now should be watered and protected against the winter winds soon to arrive.

NOVEMBER

If the ground is not already frozen, complete any and all planting and prepare gardens, trees, shrubs and evergreens for the winter. In very cold, windy areas, it is a good idea to protect evergreens and other deciduous shrubs and trees with windscreens of burlap or other material.

Once the ground is frozen, apply mulches to maintain the cold ground temperature and to prevent heaving. A good thick mulch, 3 or 4 inches in depth should be placed around plants and, if necessary, held down with stones to prevent its blowing away. Do not apply mulching materials that will pack down and mat since this will cut down on the air flow around the plant and may have disastrous results.

In warmer climates, this is the time for planting and preparing for next year as described in the September section.

DECEMBER

Enjoy a well earned rest, but don't just sit there doing nothing. Prepare for next year, via nursery catalogs and brochures. Visit your local library—you'd be amazed at the number and variety of books available. You may even accidently happen upon some new aspect of indoor or outdoor gardening that you can experiment with during the winter, and perchance even into the summer.

Walk around your property to check that your prized trees and shrubs are protected against winter's ice and wind. Make certain that large trees are "standing tall" and *stake* those that are fragile or newly planted. Brush snow from evergreens to prevent the accumulated weight from bending and then possibly breaking branches. Spray deciduous trees and shrubs and evergreens with one of the special plastic type sprays available to prevent their drying out.

Gardeners in warmer areas should now be in the work program detailed for October. But here too, the tapering off has begun, and after cleaning and protection chores are completed, its back to the books, catalogs and memories.

All over the country, this is a good time for newly experienced gardeners, no longer greenhorns, to look back on the past year's triumphs and fiascos and make plans for bigger and better adventures in gardening for the coming year.

Index